EIGHTEEN PLUS

EIGHTEEN PLUS

Unity and Diversity in Higher Education

Edited by

MARJORIE REEVES

FABER AND FABER LTD

24 Russell Square

London

First published in mcmlxv
by Faber and Faber Limited
24 Russell Square London W.C.1
Printed in Great Britain by
Latimer Trend & Co Ltd Plymouth

Contents

5

Contents

Contributors

Dame Joyce Bishop, D.B.E., formerly Headmistress, Godolphin and Latymer School, London.

James Blackie, Lecturer in Christian Ethics, University of Edinburgh.

Herbert Butterfield, Master of Peterhouse and Professor of Modern History, Cambridge.

Claude D. Curling, Lecturer in Physics, King's College, London.

Jean Floud, Fellow of Nuffield College, Oxford.

Mark Gibbs, formerly Senior History Master, Audenshaw Grammar School, Manchester.

Mary R. Glover, Director of Social Service Training, University of Keele.

Brian G. Gowenlock, Senior Lecturer in Chemistry, University of Birmingham.

Daniel Jenkins, Chaplain to the University of Sussex.

J. Maitland-Edwards, H.M.I., Staff Inspector for Chemistry.

W. R. Niblett, Dean, University of London Institute of Education.

Marjorie Reeves, Fellow of St. Anne's College, Oxford.

Geoffrey Templeman, Vice-Chancellor of the University of Kent at Canterbury.

Bryan Wilson, Reader in Sociology, University of Oxford.

Monica M. Wingate, Principal of Ball's Park Training College, Hertford.

Roger W. Young, Headmaster, George Watson's College, Edinburgh.

Preface

This book is really an extended conversation on higher education. Internal evidence will reveal that it lasted over from B.R. to A.R.—according to the new dating system. Most the main papers in it were first given at a conference in September, 1963, but were revised after the publication of the Robbins Report; some were written after Robbins. The conference was organized by the University Teachers' Group in order to extend and carry further discussions which were embodied in a previous book edited by Professor Niblett, *The Expanding University*. Here the theme has been deliberately widened to include the whole field of higher education, though it will be evident that the majority of the contributors still draw their experience from the universities.

Each writer is entirely responsible for all that appears under his or her name, but for nothing else. For all the interspersed commentary the editor alone must be held accountable. I have however, drawn heavily on the discussions which took place at the conference. Passages within quotation marks indicate that I am quoting more or less directly and I have tried to retain something of the informality of our conversations. The fact that I have been able to do this at all is due to a remarkable feat of reporting by Miss Helen Powell, supplemented by Mr. Nicholas Tyacke, to both of whom I am greatly indebted. The whole conception of the book, its themes and many of its ideas, owe a great deal, not only to the cut and thrust of the September discussions, but also to thinking which has been going on for some years in the University Teachers' Group. I am deeply grateful to many who have contributed to it. Above all, I must express my gratitude to the various contributors who so generously yielded to my persuasions first to speak and then to write. Considering the pace of existence in the post-Robbins era, it is

9

Preface

miraculous that any writing should get done at all and one knows that these essays have been produced under great pressure. The writers have strong views, sometimes in opposition to each other or the editor. They are here juxtaposed in the hope that the debate will continue.

In handling this subject terminology becomes bothersome. 'Higher education' is not an elegant form of words but there is no neat substitute for it. To gain some freedom from it I have occasionally used the phrase 'universities and colleges' as an equivalent of 'institutions of higher education', while I have consistently used the adjective *academic* to signify, not something exclusive to the universities but common to all institutions of higher education. In the essays by other contributors the context of the argument, I think, makes plain when they are thinking wholly or chiefly of universities and when more broadly of the general range of institutions.

MARJORIE REEVES

St. Anne's College
Oxford
January 1964

Note. Since this book went to press certain developments have taken place, notably with respect to the transformation of the C.A.Ts. into universities and the establishment of B.Ed. degrees. We regret that these could not be discussed here.

M. R.

Introduction

The cat is out of the bag. The simple equation Education equals Power has suddenly been grasped by the masses the world over. Power to choose your career, power to achieve the standard of living you want, power to exploit the resources of the natural world, power to control and manipulate other people—all these are seen to be conferred by Education. The emphasis in this technological age is on Power, individual, group and national. As the forms of power become increasingly complex, so the forms of education required to master their techniques become more advanced. It is astounding to reflect that, not only in developed western cultures, but in parts of the world where the witch-doctor lately held sway, the images of power are now the research-scientist, the engineer, the agricultural expert, the architect, the lawyer, the doctor, and so on. It is the army of the 'higher educated' that all states are eagerly seeking to recruit, counting their wealth in terms of 'educated potential' and aiming at all costs to catch up with their more educationally advanced rivals. It is a foothold on the ladder of the 'higher educated' that parents everywhere desire for the next generation. The role of the highly educated in this new technological age is becoming strikingly distinct: 'Ask the expert' is the instinctive response of millions in a vast variety of situations. It is a desired and respected role, but it is shared by an increasingly large number of people. Advances in the demands of society for the skills of the highly-trained and the demands of the young to acquire these are revolutionizing the proportions in which they stand to the rest of society. Thus the concept of the *élite* is no longer one of a minority, either closed or open, and yet, curiously enough, the Gilbert and Sullivan law, 'When everyone is somebody, then no one's anybody', does not seem to be working out: the ever-increasing numbers of the highly-trained simply demonstrate that society can do with more and more 'somebodies'. Thus, on the one hand, the 'experts' are being drawn from a much wider range of society and, on the other, their action penetrates much more deeply into it. A whole new category is being born into society.

From this perspective the army of the young entering upon higher education is much more united in its common experiences *vis-à-vis* society than it is diversified in its various types of training. Viewed by the rest of the community, all these young people have the brains and the opportunity which will give them power: they will enter the category of the experts and be listened to, they will be able to manipulate things and people, they will, to greater or less extent, choose their careers and move about, even internationally, in a society of those with a similar expertise. They may well slough off one whole social environment and assume another. For the student, the whole experience is a disturbing, even though exhilarating, one: he has to come to terms with his own powers, greater or smaller, he has to accept the responsibilities which mastery in any field brings, he has to learn that, in some sense, higher education—the acquisition of expertise of a high order—draws a line which separates him from the rest. He may have to suffer the woes of the *déracinés* and yet, if he is to live healthily in a healthy society, he must rediscover his solidarity with the whole community. In a very fundamental sense the experiences and the problems of being a student are the same, whether his course be in a college of advanced technology, a university or a college of education.

This is a whole new situation and it demands a whole new understanding of higher education—of the relationship of its institutions to society, of the total experience to which we subject students, of their vocation when they return to society. We need a proper concept of higher education in its unity. It forms a distinct and radical experience for the student; it plays a decisive role in society. There is an important distinction to be drawn between *higher* education and *further* education. In stressing the unity of higher education we are drawing a line which separates it sharply from other forms of continued education. But here at once we find ourselves in a dilemma. For in order to penetrate its special problems we must think deeply about this special category of persons undergoing this special educational experience. Yet the last thing we wish to do is to draw a permanent line of distinction between these persons and the rest. On the one hand, their distinguishing experience is only valid if it sends them back into society with a warmer desire to understand and to belong, but, on the other, we have failed unless it is a really distinctive experience.

To a large extent the discussions in this book revolve round this dilemma and the ways of resolving it. We must think of the institutions of higher education as the instruments of social policy and yet ask, How far are the demands of society identical with its needs? We must examine the 'student experience' as something unique, and yet remember that each student has a specific *habitat* in his community. Broadly speaking, in relation to their society, the needs of all young people in higher education are the same: all need a fruitful relationship to the previous generation, an understanding of their own generation and a grasp of their responsibility—at varying levels—as leaders in the society to be. In this sense of common needs the unity of higher education is a basic assumption of this book.

M. R.

Part One

HIGHER EDUCATION
AND SOCIETY

There never was a time when higher education was not, in some sense, an answer to social need: the medieval university, for instance, combined a strong drive to seek knowledge for the glory of God with a definite vocational bias towards those professions most needed—law, medicine, the Church. Equally, there never was a time when sociological factors were not built into these institutions through the mere presence of their members, however privileged and withdrawn from outside pressures those members sought to be. The revolution of today lies, first, in the conscious grasp of higher education as almost the most effective instrument of social policies and, secondly, in the focus of public attention upon it, both in terms of ambition for the next generation and of eager interest in all its affairs. It is a commonplace, but still an astounding one, that universities are such front-page news. The 'university of the air' entices professors out of hiding-places, student quizzes on television are discussed in Lyons Corner-Houses, student discipline attracts an understandable but embarrassing degree of publicity, while student magazines are often read much more widely than they ought to be. Of course the advent of mass media accounts in part for the revolution in publicity, but the professors are surprisingly willing to emerge and student news is only fed to the public because its appetite is avid. Long before the Robbins Report, dons were in dialogue with the public on the issue of expansion and the student image was beginning to compete with the pop. figures in public interest. It is fascinating to see the universities and the public, as it were, rushing into each other's embrace and ultimately this kindling of interest and concern on both sides ought to be fruitful in terms of a clearer understanding of what higher education is for. But the very involvement of higher education in society intensifies the problem of right relationships. These must be discussed in terms of both institutions and persons.

Should the institutions of higher education be moulded in each age directly to the demands of society? Or perhaps the question has to be Can they avoid being so moulded? And yet one may still ask Ought they to be *readily* malleable or ought they—for the sake of society itself—to attempt to preserve an abiding, more resistant core? Mrs. Floud analyses the sociological factors which press on universities and colleges today.

M. R.

The Demands of Society

JEAN FLOUD

———————

The programme of this conference announces that I am to talk about 'the *demands* of society', whilst Dr. Wilson has as his topic 'the *needs* of students, and Dr. Templeman as his 'the *responsibilities* of institutions of higher education'. Society makes demands, students have needs, and universities must define their responsibilities. The implicit problem provides a popular *point d'appui* for the opposition in the debate over expansion. I should like to take a closer look, not at the problem itself, but at the assumption which seems to underlie it; namely, that the forces responsible for the latest 'crisis in the universities' are, in some fairly straightforward sense, external forces—'The Demands of Society': the thirst for degrees and the demand for ever larger numbers of adequately taught administrators, scientists and technologists.

I think the picture is much more complicated than this. The universities have always had to earn their right to serve the academic values by training men and women for the professions. It is true that, for a variety of reasons, they are today being asked to take on much more under this head than ever before; more than many in the universities think they can manage. But there is more to it than that, and in examining this notion of the demands of society I want to suggest that it is an illusion to suppose that if the thirst for degrees or the demand for professional man-power could be largely satisfied outside the universities, leaving them to expand 'only at the growing point of knowledge',[1] this latest crisis in the universities would be disposed of. The explosion of numbers is matched by the explosion of knowledge. The nature of the scientific enterprise is being transformed by new techniques of producing knowledge; by the growth of a complex division of labour in the sciences and a large increase in the necessary scale of investment. Society today demands new knowledge as well as new men; the state is as interested in the higher learning as in higher education, in investing in science as in investing in men.

It is doubtful if the 'nationalization of the intellect'[1] could be avoided by resisting the democratization of higher education; or that the university as an academic community could be saved from eclipse by a policy of 'expanding only at the growing points of knowledge'.

The idea of the university as a community of older and younger scholars, devoted to the combined and closely related activities of teaching and research, underlies the distinctively English pattern of university organization.[2] Our idea is to admit a relatively small number of carefully selected young people to a university community, preferably residential, in which the proportion of teachers to pupils and the organization of studies are such as to ensure remarkably low drop-out and failure rates. The higher education of those destined for the profession, and the preparation and recruitment of the academic succession are carried out in the same context of higher learning. University education is the privilege of a minority comprised, in part, of the offspring of well-to-do or influential parents, but today largely of young people whose talents, regardless of social background, entitle them to an expensive subsidy from public funds.

This idea of the university and this idea of higher education are now under attack. The view is widespread that the university is the apex of a national system of education based in the primary schools. Intending students and their parents see the university neither as a community of scholars nor even, any longer, as a place in which to spend three priceless years of prolonged adolescence; it is a place of higher education in which one prepares for a career and in which one's prowess is acknowledged with the award of a degree.

It is this view which constitutes the threat concealed in numbers—in the thirst for degrees and the expansion to meet it. Of course, numbers in themselves generate immense problems of staffing, standards, and organization. The crucial problem, however, is not one of growth, but democratization: by which is meant, not that a relatively small number of university places

are competed for on equal intellectual terms by young people
regardless of their social origin, but that the universities absorb
a much larger fraction of the total of young people aged 18–21
than has hitherto been thought either desirable or possible; so
high a proportion, in fact, as to make the experience of a university education no longer a privilege but a commonplace.

This process has gone far in America,[3] where between 1940
and the present day, the proportion of the 18-year-old age-
group attending college has risen dramatically, from just under
one-sixth to something like two-fifths, and where there seems
every reason to suppose that by 1970 the figure will have risen
to one-half.

There are, of course, a hundred particular ways in which the
American situation cannot be compared with our own and used
as a basis of prediction for development in this country. But
there is one crucial general respect in which we do not differ
and which makes this remarkable development relevant for us.
Both America and this country are advanced industrial
societies, some would prefer to say, post-industrial, or technological societies. Their economies depend on the application of
science to technology; the scale of enterprise is very large; there
is accordingly (quite apart from military considerations) a
built-in incentive to expand markets and to sustain the momentum of technological advance by institutionalizing innovation
and investing heavily and continuously in science and scientific
man-power. Hence the insatiable demand for educated talent
characteristic of these societies; and hence the development in
them of a labour force in which, not only do black-coated
workers predominate, but within this broad group, the clerical
and kindred workers created by the inter-war expansion of
secondary education are gradually taking second place to the
increasingly influential and numerous group of professional and
technical workers produced by the post-war expansion in
higher education.[4] The harsh and distasteful reality is that education, and especially higher education, has become part of the
economic foundations of modern society. It is this profound
transformation in the social function of education that underlies the present 'crisis in the universities'.

The democratization of higher education is an important
element in this crisis; it produces the twin problems of numbers
and 'the new student' which dominate current debate. But it

is far from being the only, or even the most important element. The same social forces are responsible for a more insidious and less generally acknowledged threat to the traditional idea of the university, in the shape of the radical changes they bring about in the character of the academic profession.

The new student confronts the new teacher and both are products of the same social development. If we are in danger of neglecting the problem of the new teacher, to which I will return shortly, we are equally in danger, it seems to me, of misunderstanding the problem of the new student.

The new student is regarded as the main importer into the university of subversive utilitarian and vocational attitudes towards his studies. This is sometimes taken as an indication that he has not been selected rigorously enough, that 'more means worse' or that we are 'scraping the barrel'. A more enlightened view supposes these attitudes to be a simple reflection of his background. It is argued that he has come up the hard way; that his parents will have had at most no more than a secondary education; that although able, he is not so able that his climb has been effortless; that he is the victim of early specialization and has blinkered himself in order to clear the major examination hurdles at 11 plus or 18 plus; that he has had no chance to make good at school the cultural deficiencies of his family background.

All this is true enough; their changed social composition does present universities with problems of social and intellectual assimilation which are novel, at least in scale. It is a mistake, however, to suppose that these problems are or will be generally confined to students of humble origin. The vocationalizing of education is endemic to scientific industrialism. Technological society puts a premium on the value of education in the labour market; as the division of labour becomes ever more complex, vocationalism in education will become increasingly widespread. A utilitarian and vocational attitude to education will not be confined to students of low socio-economic origin, even though it is probably true, and quite comprehensible that it should be true, that the incidence of these attitudes is higher among these students. Modern students are, in the nature of things, bound to be increasingly vocational and utilitarian in their approach to education, regardless of their background; this is not because everyone is corrupted by twentieth-

22

century mass society, but because the economic and social role of education in technological society is such that everybody's aspirations centre upon it, as those of former generations centred naturally on income and career. Education is the turning point of everybody's life today. Scientific industrialism swells the professional schools in the universities, populates them with students drawn from the nation at large, and swamps the academic community.

There are those who believe that the number of people fitted for a university education is very small, and that the educational problem presented by the new student is soluble, if at all, only on entirely uneconomic terms as regards both money and time taken off research for teaching him. Hence the use of metaphors like 'the margin of cultivation' and the raising of awkward questions such as 'is he really worth it?'. But there are others who feel strongly about the social and intellectual responsibilities of the university, who would like to give an education in university style to all the public-service professions, new as well as old, major as well as minor.[4] In the university, training and instruction are converted into an education through the consideration of general ideas and through critical inspection of the intellectual suppositions which underlie professional thought and practice. But on what basis can we determine the university's responsibility to one profession rather than another? The professions are increasing alarmingly in number with the development of industrialism. How can we defend the willingness of the universities to embrace the law, medicine, the Church, the senior Civil Service, but to give a lukewarm and reluctant reception to education and a cold shoulder to business and even to social administration? And if the newer or the lesser professions are in fact adopted whole-heartedly by the universities, can the academic community possibly survive in institutions on the scale that this development would presuppose and make necessary? Surely the tail will inevitably come to wag the dog?

These are delicate problems, but I do not think they represent the essence of our current difficulties. If it were really only a question of numbers and of a less well-prepared and suitably motivated student body, we should find a way out although the decisions to be taken as to the allocation of resources might be painful. The situation is intrinsically complicated, however, by the changes which are simultaneously taking place in the position of the university teacher, the effect of which is to imperil the quantity or the quality, or both, of his teaching just when the demand for inspired, devoted and technically resourceful teaching is at its maximum. Democratization changes the social background of the academic as of the other professions recruited from the universities; and the incorporation of science into modern government makes for the divorce of teaching from research over wide areas of academic life.

In a growing number of instances, both teacher and student come from the same humble background and have climbed the same educational ladder. This trend will obviously continue and I suspect that it is already a commonplace in the United States. Mobility through education has many interesting implications for the academic profession. Here I am concerned with the similarity of background between teacher and pupil. This may mean simply that both are tainted with utilitarian vocational values—except that, in the case of the teacher, they are masked by his nominal membership of the academic community. His teaching may be a job like anyone else's and in his heart he may be immune to the academic ethos. Or it may mean that both are in some degree socially uprooted. Here there are two possibilities and there is no reason in either case to suppose that the common dilemma will make for mutual understanding. The new teacher may be as over-assimilated to the academic ethos as the new student is under-assimilated. I leave aside the possibility in this case (which I believe to be more frequent than we might like to think) that he may manifest unpleasant signs of cultural arrogance in his educational mission—seeking to indoctrinate students with the more superficial cultural conventions of an *élite* to which he himself is a newcomer. Perhaps more important is the possibility that he may manifest quite severe signs of irritation and impatience with his students. The University Grants Committee in one of its annual reports has noticed what is a familiar experience in the common-rooms, that the severest strictures on the new student come from the younger teachers. It would be worth investigating the relevance of variables other than age to this problem. Another danger is that the teacher may be insecurely, rather than over-assimilated. In this case he may be very ill at ease or may tend to transmit his own 'cultural bilingualism' to his students and thereby the form rather than the substance of the distinctive academic tradition that he is supposed to represent and to personify. This is the Trojan horse within the walls.

The incorporation of science into modern government, the change in its status from being an instrument to being an object of public policy, is the result of advances in military technology over the past half-century and of the more recent growth of state economic and social planning. This development is still in its early stages in this country but that it is under way cannot be doubted. The setting up of National Scientific Advisory Committees and the provision of public funds for scientific research puts new pressures on the universities, whether by diverting talent from the academic profession into specialized research bodies outside the universities or by introducing into the universities a disastrous conflict between the claims of teaching and research.[5]

The problem can be seen in an acute form in America where there has recently occurred both a tremendous growth in the numbers of students and an unprecedented flow of federal funds into scientific and technological research.[6] Graduate institutions flourish at the expense of undergraduate institutions and gifted scientists may be cut off altogether from teaching, which is increasingly undertaken by the more mediocre and pedestrian members of the profession. And lest it be thought that this development in the sciences does not strike at the heart of the university, it is well to remind ourselves of what Professor Michael Fogarty has dubbed the Myth of the Arts Majority. 'Deep in the subconscious of a surprising number of university people, let alone of people outside,' he writes, 'is buried the belief that the typical academic man studies English or History or Classics, and that people in fields directly interchanging with the more profitable professions outside are an exception and a minority. The truth is very different. The typical modal member of a university staff practises a science-based technology (40 per cent), in close contact with members of related professions outside. The next largest group (27 per cent) is in pure science. A third group, the social scientists (9 per cent), increasingly share the characteristics of pure and applied science not only in their methods of work but in their relation to professions outside.'[7]

It is a far cry under these conditions to the idea of the university advanced by Lord James to an earlier conference in this series when he described it as 'a community where teachers and taught discuss, evaluate and investigate difficult, and sometimes original ideas of considerable generality.'[8] But the tide of development cannot be turned, even in the English universities, and we must come to terms with it.

I do not at all mean by this that we should abandon the idea of the university as an academic community. It seems essential, however, to face the seemingly ineluctable social, economic and political forces which beset it with our eyes open. As university teachers we must be vigilant and resourceful—and self-critical: able even under the pressures of rapid growth and changing function to distinguish ancient and honourable scruples from the newly-acquired vanities of a threatened *élite*. We are notorious for our lack of curiosity about our own affairs (the scientific validity of selection procedures, for instance) and our readiness to fly in the face of facts when they touch our pride (e.g. facts about the predictive value of interviews). If we are sincere in our devotion to the idea of the university as an academic community we shall seek to banish our ignorance of ourselves and encourage the application of social research to our problems of planning and development;[9] we shall seek by means of systematic self-scrutiny and enlightened experiment to sustain and revitalize the traditional idea under the new conditions. For if technological society 'demands' educated experts and a continuous flow of new knowledge, who can doubt that it 'needs' the academic community?

NOTES

1. Dr. David Thomson, 'Academic Cats and Dogs', *The Cambridge Review* (March 1963).

2. See 'British Universities' by A. H. Halsey, *European Journal of Sociology*, III, 1 (1962).

3. See Martin Trow, 'The Democratisation of Higher Education in America', *European Journal of Sociology*, III, 2 (1962).

4. B. R. Clark presents a useful discussion of all these points in *Educating the Expert Society* (Chandler Publishing Company. San Francisco, 1963).

5. See A. H. Halsey, 'Science and Government', *Minerva* (Autumn, 1963).

6. Harold Orlans, *The Effects of Federal Programmes on Higher Education* (Brookings Institution, 1962).

7. M. Fogarty, 'A Society of Equal Colleagues', *British Universities Annual* (1963), p. 78. I have added the percentages in brackets which are taken from Table 12, Appendix Three of the Robbins Report, p. 17.

8. *The Expanding University*, ed. W. R. Niblett, p. 38 (Faber and Faber, London, 1962).

9. See Sir Eric Ashby's Presidential Address to the British Association, 'Investment in Man', *The Advancement of Science*, XX, 85 (1963).

The preceding paper raises acutely the question of whether society's demands from higher education are the same as its needs. Who are the academics to set themselves up as guides and consciences of society? They live under the same pressures and influences as other men; they are subject to the same corruptions. Pride, greed, envy, cannot be barred admittance to academy places. Moreover, there are peculiar academic forms of sin as well as all the common ones. Yet perhaps it is true that temptations to special vices are always matched by opportunities for special virtues and to acknowledge our sins, both corporate and individual, does not relieve academics of responsibility to safeguard by their practice certain permanent values in the community. Because it is almost impossible to say this without priggishness, we try to evade a truth which is thrust at us. We take cover behind our 'conditioning', our ordinariness, the common elements in our experience. All this is true and good to be expressed, yet there is one peculiar circumstance, at least, of academic living that is visible to any casual eye: very few other sections of the community work surrounded by books. This alone surely ought to give a perspective on the needs of society which can contribute uniquely to its life. 'To whom much is given, from him much will be required' applies with special force here, and it is nonsense to pretend that academic institutions and persons are not required to exercise special responsibilities in relation to the rest of the community. The longer perspective imparted by learning is often thought to make conservatives, but in fact seems to produce as many radicals; either way, however, it ought to train in awareness of fundamental needs and values in human society. Thus academic responsibility must be seen as an age-long duty to meet changing social needs without losing sight of abiding principles. Has this happened in the past? Can it happen today? Dr. Templeman discusses these questions in his paper.

M.R.

29

2

The Responsibilities of Institutions of Higher Education

GEOFFREY TEMPLEMAN

At the outset I should explain that I have rather arbitrarily narrowed the scope of my title by confining myself to universities and particularly to the British universities. I have done this, not because I do not recognize the importance of the contribution to higher education made in this country and elsewhere by non-university institutions, but because my own experience and competence, such as they are, only allow me to speak of universities.

To deal with this subject at all is to give hostages to fortune, for so much has been written about it lately with no very obvious effect. I have only ventured to grapple with the matter at all because I believe that a more work-a-day approach than has hitherto been tried may yield results of interest, and even of value. Thus I do not want to discuss the matter on a theoretical level in terms of first principles. Rather I want first to inquire what is actually being done, and what general, if unavowed idea of university duty, this implies. Beyond that I shall ask how far this general, if unavowed, conception of university duty meets what is now needed of universities. If it should then emerge that what is now being done falls short of what is needed, I shall ask what might be done about the discrepancy.

As is often the case, the realities of the present can best be discerned in the light of the past. This is particularly true of universities. Universities as we know them are a medieval invention, and viewed in the context of their 700-odd years of history, it is clear that in a fundamental sense universities have an unchanging duty. This duty is so important that, if for any reason a university has failed to discharge it, then that institution has ceased to be a university in anything but name. This duty can be summarily defined as the job of adding to knowledge and disseminating it at the highest level as effectively as possible, freely and without external constraint. Very early in their history, the European universities almost instinctively felt their way to this general idea of their duty. When the Masters of Paris escaped from the confines of Notre Dame and settled on the Left Bank on the Mont. St. Genevieve, they were trying to escape from the suffocating effects of ecclesiastical authority on the work they were seeking to do. The formidable array of privileges and exemptions from royal and ecclesiastical authority with which all the medieval universities hurried to arm themselves, had the same purpose. They were intended to allow universities to work freely and without external interference. How successful they were in this endeavour is neatly illustrated in the remark attributed to Pope Boniface VIII. In a moment of exasperation he said to the Doctors of the University of Paris, 'You sit in chairs and think that Christ is ruled by your reasoning.' The right to academic autonomy, though nowadays far less heavily buttressed by legal sanctions than it used to be, is no less vital to us than it was to our medieval predecessors.

Similarly the primary duty of adding to knowledge has been accepted by universities from the beginning. It is true that the way in which thirteenth-century scholars thought of adding to knowledge is very different from the manner in which we now conceive it should be done. Nevertheless, it would be wrong to suppose that the scholastics of the thirteenth century, within the limits of their day and age, were not as concerned to add to knowledge as are, for example, the scientists of our own time. In teaching, too, the same is true, although needs and methods have changed over the centuries. Cynics may well say these have not changed as much as perhaps they ought to have done in some directions.

From a very different standpoint all this is no less evident. There are numerous past instances of universities squeezed by civil and ecclesiastical pressure to the point at which independence of mind was no longer possible so that learning died and teaching decayed. Then nothing remained but a university in name from which the spirit and purpose had fled away. When in 1411 Archbishop Arundel visited Oxford to root out the remnants of Wyclif's teaching he destroyed the intellectual vigour of that university as effectively as Hitler and his accomplices put an end for the time being to science and learning in the German universities.

Decay can also come from within. Then the spirit of free inquiry falters or is crushed by indolence or indifference on the part of those who have the duty both to advance knowledge and to disseminate it. The kind of lethargy that beset the English universities in the eighteenth century has its parallel in the history of other universities at other times. This state of affairs has also frequently involved something else of great importance. If it is evident that in a real sense the universities' duty is an unchanging one, it is no less true that this responsibility has to be discharged in changing social and intellectual circumstances. This makes it necessary for universities to be sensitive to these changes, and to undertake the even more difficult task of adapting to them. The history of universities proves over and over again how hard and irksome this adaptation has often revealed itself to be.

For our present purpose it is worth looking with some attention at the last major adaptation to changed social and intellectual circumstances which the English universities made. It happened in a reluctant, piecemeal and rather painful way and was spread over roughly the last half of last century. Even now it is not generally recognized for what it was. Many people are content to note that in that period what is still usually called the reform of Oxford and Cambridge took place, and side by side with this the first generation of civic universities came to birth. In fact the changes then brought about were sufficiently momentous to be worth calling the Academic Revolution of the Nineteenth Century. This revolution involved the achievement of three things. First, there was a significant widening of the curriculum in universities to give pride of place to the sciences. Secondly, there was renewed and very heavy emphasis on the duty of research in universities, and particularly on the duty of research in the sciences whereby additions might be made to useful knowledge. Thirdly, effective teaching was established in a much larger number of separate disciplines, some of them very new. It is unnecessary to explain in detail here why these changes came about when they did. It is sufficient to say that they represent the successful outcome of heavy pressure on the universities to adapt themselves to the then evident social, intellectual and economic needs of society. Like so many Victorian achievements, this academic revolution has received far less attention than it deserves. Certainly it would repay closer study than it has hitherto had for the light it can cast upon our present predicament. For us its significance lies in a single fact. The changes then made solidified into a notion of university duty which has been carried forward to our own time, and which is the general, if unavowed standard, by which we now measure our academic responsibilities and in the light of which we seek to discharge them.

The history of the English universities in the present century presents a curious dichotomy. On the one hand there has been an immense and creative flowering of research, particularly in the sciences, and it is in the universities that some of the most significant advances in fundamental knowledge have been made in our time. Yet in their methods of government and, even more important, in their notions of what a university ought to do in teaching and research, the English universities have accepted the ideas of their Victorian forebears and practised them almost without question down to the present time.

Much of the criticism and heart-searching about what universities are now doing compared with what some think they ought to do, comes from a widespread realization of this fact. Many argue that what is generally called over-specialization in undergraduate courses has been carried to absurd lengths, and propose various radical alternatives which would have the effect of destroying the pattern of first degree studies with which we have become familiar over the last half-century. Others, particularly those in universities, tend to blame the schools and especially the character of present sixth-form teaching. It is argued that by the time boys and girls reach the university, they are so far set in specialist ways that nothing can be done to change them. These and other criticisms are familiar enough, but, in practice, they have not proved very effective because they are too superficial.

It might be worth illustrating this point at rather greater length by using undergraduate studies in their present form as an example. The characteristic feature of modern English undergraduate teaching is the single subject specialized Honours course. This was a Victorian innovation made with a double

C   33

purpose. First it had the laudable object of raising the level of undergraduate attainment, and second it was also designed to establish a number of comparatively new subjects in their own right. These two purposes have been carried forward to the present. It is true that the pattern of undergraduate studies in English universities is now infinitely more complicated than it was at the beginning of the century, but it is essentially the same pattern. There are many more specialized branches of study available to undergraduates than there were fifty years ago, but the structure and pattern of each of these branches is the same as it used to be. If anything, particular branches of study open to undergraduates are now much more self-sufficient than they were.

This is something which comes within the experience of those of us whose concern with university teaching is comparatively short. Since the end of the last war there seems to have been a marked tendency for the shedding of subsidiary studies in many specialized courses open to undergraduates. The practice, almost universal, down to the end of the 1930's, whereby an undergraduate reading history, for example, was required to study another language and another related subject at least for one year, has in many cases now been abandoned, and the tendency is for the whole period of study to be concentrated more and more upon those things that can be brought within the conventional category of history. Teachers, too, have also restricted their range. Many departments are now staffed by specialists in a way that was not the case even twenty years ago. These specialists tend more and more to concentrate not only in their research, where it is perfectly proper so to do, but in their teaching also, upon the narrow field of their personal interests. Thus the student is confronted with an ever-narrowing course, with one which grows heavier as knowledge increases and with one presented to him by a team of specialists each shut up within the confines of his own limited concern.

It is easy to state the case in this way, but it is also necessary to recognize that this development is an honest attempt to grapple with two very intractable facts. The first, a familiar one, is the great and continuing growth of knowledge in practically every discipline. The second is of a rather different kind. Experience seems to show that study in depth is essential for the achievement of the kind of mastery of a subject required at

34

university level. In practice this means that at some point in his course every undergraduate, if only for a brief time, ought to stop relying entirely on second-hand information and opinions. He must make at least a brief visit, as it were, to the front, to the edge of knowledge in his subject, to discover what conditions are really like there.

If these things are so, then it is clear that the backbone of undergraduate studies in the future must be formed as it is now by an element of rigorous specialization. For only in this way is it possible to ensure a continuing supply of the university specialists without which our society cannot maintain, let alone improve, itself. The real question we have to ask is whether it is any longer possible, in present circumstances, to accept specialist training in various forms as the sole duty a university owes to its undergraduates.

It is pertinent to ask this question. The social situation in which universities have to work has changed out of all recognition since the beginning of the century, and major alterations have happened most noticeably since the end of the second war. Perhaps this can be best illustrated by means of a contrast. What has earlier been called the academic revolution of the nineteenth century in England was a rather painful adjustment by universities to new social circumstances. In the last thirty years of last century it gradually became clear to those concerned that the sciences would henceforth need to bulk large in the work of universities both in teaching and research. This was simply because it was becoming obvious that a modern industrial society was having to depend to an increasing extent upon the enlargement and dissemination of scientific knowledge. This being so, universities gradually disposed themselves to meet the new need, but it was a need they could meet within clearly defined boundaries. Then most of their students and their staff were drawn from the middle and professional classes. They came from homes and schools where it could be assumed they had already received their education in the wider sense of that word. They also came from a society where standards and values were much less in question than is now the case. Thus, at the end of last century, universities were fully justified in thinking that so far as undergraduates were concerned, their task was the limited one of providing the kind of specialist training with which we are familiar. They did not have to concern themselves with the education of their students in the wider sense, for this was something which was looked after elsewhere. Of course in one way this is too simple an explanation of what happened. There were other compelling reasons of a quite different kind to encourage universities to concern themselves almost entirely with specialist study.

In part the development of specialist study for undergraduates grew out of a then manifest need to establish a wide range of new subjects each in its own right. The major arts subjects, history, English literature, French language and literature in particular are examples of independent branches of study which, in the form we now know them, are of comparatively recent development. They owe their present shape and progress largely to the fact that they made their appearance as separate disciplines in universities toward the end of last century. The same thing is true of the main branches of the physical, the biological and the engineering sciences. All took their present shape and owe much of their modern development to their establishment as accepted university disciplines in the latter part of last century. Moreover this point goes deeper still. The process is continually repeated, and now in what we are learning to call the social sciences, a whole new group of subjects are being established in their own right in much the same sort of way that the major disciplines in the humanities and the natural sciences were established in universities almost a hundred years ago. Nor does the process stop with the establishment of a new subject in its own right. From among those who are trained in it as an undergraduate discipline and then proceed to further work in research will come the scholars and scientists who build up the established body of knowledge in the subject still further, develop its techniques and root it even more firmly in the intellectual landscape.

Yet when all this is said and done, the fact remains that it is the kind of concept of university duty, which was established particularly in regard to undergraduate studies in the great changes made toward the end of last century in the English universities, that has produced the kind of situation with which we are now familiar. As has been briefly indicated, these changes were the outcome of an adjustment to manifest social and intellectual needs when they were made. The contrast mentioned above emerges clearly when we consider the extent to which the manifest social and educational needs of our own time require, if not a radical change, at least some considerable additions to this concept of university duty, particularly in the matter of undergraduate training, which we have inherited from our Victorian forebears, through our own initiative enlarged, and still continue to practise with great vigour.

That our society has a voracious appetite for new knowledge which can be put to practical use is a commonplace which hardly bears repetition. Yet this has been the greatest single influence in transforming the modern situation of our universities. In particular it has dragged them from the edge to the centre of public concern simply because they, in the nature of things, have a large share not merely in producing new knowledge, but above all in training those who can be both the producers of new knowledge and the agents by which it is put to practical use. We are in process of becoming irretrievably professionalized, on a scale that is without precedent and in a way which is fraught with the largest and most serious social consequences. The long reign of the amateur is quickly drawing to its close; although there are still many amateurs about, they are steadily being elbowed out by the professionals, by those, that is to say, elaborately prepared and trained not so much for a particular occupation as for the job of dealing with this or that technology, whether it be in industry or medicine, or, if this is not stretching the meaning of the word too far, in teaching itself at all levels.

Whether they like it or not, the universities have the job of producing the *élite* of these new professionals. It is often objected by those blinded by egalitarian prejudice, that universities are over-concerned with the privileged, the *élite*. This is a criticism entirely misplaced, since in the nature of things it is the business of universities, not merely traditionally but ineluctably in present circumstances, to deal with the minority who are capable of being trained and developed to the highest attainable level. We need to face the fact that there are basic, inbuilt inequalities which have to be reckoned with and used. From now on these new professionals, whose leaders will have been trained in the universities, will steadily climb up in virtue of their technical expertise to positions of major responsibility in every branch of our national life. Some of them will sit by the levers of power, and this is unavoidable since they alone will have the kind of knowledge and background required to manage society in its new infinitely more technically developed form. Yet although great power may come to the engineer, the biologist, the social scientist and the others in virtue of their specialist knowledge and accomplishments, this does not mean that they are thereby automatically fitted to undertake the full responsibilities of those who will have not merely to say how to do things, but will have to make the infinitely harder decisions as to what ought to be done and what is worth doing. The real menace of our present situation is that the graduate adequately trained in his specialty is likely to find himself forced by the exigencies of our new social and economic circumstances to a dominant situation in society, where he will also be required to act as a leader of opinion. In this capacity he must know, as has just been said, not merely how to do things but what is worth doing. The likelihood is that his academic training and his technical expertise will by themselves be of little use to him in facing this new range of problems. He will then rightly look back upon his university training and reflect, when it is too late, that while it gave him much in the way of professional preparation, it almost entirely neglected to equip him in a more general way; in fact to educate him in the wider sense of the word. That this will have happened, will, as he will clearly see, have to be directly attributed to the limited notion of university duty which is now in fashion.

Yet this is not the whole of the size of our modern dilemma. Universities now draw their students from the whole range of the social classes in a way that has never happened before. This is a very modern development. It really began after the end of the second war, and there is good reason for thinking that the true social revolution of our time is not connected with the Welfare State at all, but with the opening of opportunities for higher education to the whole range of the ablest in the community whatever their social origin. This is not primarily the outcome of a desire for gratifying the urge for wider opportunity for talent. It is true that this consideration has entered into it, but in retrospect it may well seem that the real, if not the clearly acknowledged, reason for doing what has been done in this matter in this country in the last twenty years lay elsewhere. It lay in the not very clear recognition that in the new situation in which we as a people found ourselves our real and continuing shortage was not of dollars, or oil, or coal, but of brains; in short, that to hold our own, let alone develop ourselves, we needed to make the fullest use of intelligence wherever it was to be found. For this reason the ladders were set up so that boys and girls could have at least the possibility, wherever they came from, granted that they possessed the necessary capacity, of climbing up into the universities and there securing for themselves the kind of training which would enable them to take hold of the advantages as well as discharging the new duties to be laid upon them. One of the inescapable effects of this kind of development, although since it happens over a period its effects are only slowly obvious, is that what can, without too much exaggeration, be called a new aristocracy is in process of being created. This aristocracy, recruited deliberately from the whole range of society, may be in a measure self-perpetuating, but it will be constantly renewed by additions made through the rigid system of educational selection we have devised and are now operating with a ruthlessness which appals at least some foreigners. It may well mean that we, by acting in this way, manage to deprive every other social group of its natural leaders, and we may well produce for ourselves before too long a society almost Byzantine-like in its acquiescence.

Without pressing these—to some minds nightmarish—possibilities too far, it still remains true that the much larger number of graduates of the immediate future will need to have a wider kind of university training than their predecessors could manage with.

This is reinforced by yet another consideration. Our society is much less sure of itself in the matter of standards and values than was the case even fifty years ago. There is now far less agreement even than there was then on these matters. In part at least this is to be ascribed to the intense drive for material improvement which has characterized our society of late, and to the great prestige which has been accorded to what the eighteenth century used to call useful knowledge. There are other reasons too, such as the dislocation of war and all the moral and social upheaval which has been brought about by the age of calamity in which we have lived. These corrosive things have in general led to the widespread decay of religious observance and to the wholesale abandonment of traditional morality, but in the academic field in particular they have had a very malign effect. The humane sciences, history, philosophy and literature have in their modern development all shown the effects of the spirit of the age. There has been what it is not too fanciful to describe as a widespread loss of faith by those concerned in the worthwhileness and validity of their studies. This is perhaps most evident in philosophy where self-questioning and self-distrust has, or so it seems to a layman, brought the subject to the edge of bankruptcy. The historians have turned away in many cases from the great issues presented by their subject to immerse themselves in technical trivialities. They have forgotten that history is human experience spread out in time, and only remembered that it is very important to get research techniques straight.

There is little to be gained by lamentation over what is, to say the least of it, an alarming situation, but there is one thing which would seem very clear. It is that at the undergraduate level universities must feel themselves to have a rather larger obligation than at present they do. They have somehow to contrive things so that they give the appropriate specialist training, which must be furnished, but to that they have also to add some measure of what, for want of a better word, must be called education. To put it bluntly, no university in present circumstances ought any longer to be content to allow those of its students who graduate in the natural sciences to go out into the world without some adult awareness at least of the wider implications of their science. Similarly it would seem equally necessary that no university should continue to allow its graduates in non-science subjects to leave without at least an intelligent understanding of the rudiments of the scientific attitude and approach and of the kind of impact that the sciences have made, are making and will in increasing measure continue to make upon the society in which they themselves will have to live and work.

All this is really a plea for an enlargement of our existing notion of university duty. An enlargement which it is very difficult to make, but an enlargement which is inescapably necessary. It would not be appropriate here to suggest what might be done in any way but in the barest outline. The main concern of this short essay has been to try to argue that the need is there. At the moment there is not as widespread a recognition of this fact as the need of the times demands. Perhaps it might just be worth adding this final comment. If there is in the next few years a growing realization in universities of this need to widen the notion of their duty toward undergraduates, this will have to be accompanied by some genuine difficult experiment in how the need is to be met. It may be guessed, from what little experience is already to hand, that this need will not be met, except to a very limited extent, by direct instruction. It is much more likely to be satisfied in a host of indirect ways, and perhaps most importantly by development on a much larger scale than has hitherto been possible in universities of the kind of social mixing which effectively planned residence allows. It is not simply because there is a shortage of lodgings that the new universities particularly are insistent upon the need for residence. They see clearly that if the kind of educational job which now needs to be done is to be done for the next generation of undergraduates, then residence is part of the essential physical plant for the doing of that job.

So far we have been discussing chiefly the relation of academic institutions to society. But there is also the immediate human problem of the student and his community. Every student, as we have already said, has a *habitat*. Already it is true to say that many students never leave it, and if problems of expansion are met, as may have urged, by a vast increase of non-resident provision, or by correspondence courses, or by a return to a more localized type of institution, it will become the common experience to be a student without any great change of social environment. Yet many academic administrators and teachers have fought passionately for the residential academic community as fundamental to the student experience, and many would even now maintain that the lesser of two evils is to give bread to a smaller number rather than a stone to the larger. Yet again, on the other side, it is argued that this is not a question of bread or stones: the 'bread' of student diet is not so precious that it cannot be eaten in ordinary company or salted by common conversation. Do students need to be taken out of their immediate social environment in order to prepare them for their role in the future society? Is the academic enterprise which they undertake essentially 'monastic' in the sense that it can only be fully experienced in a withdrawn community dedicated to this activity? Most students would laugh such a concept to scorn, but this does not make the question any less real. Expansion may force us to dilute what we offer, but this does not relieve us of the urgent duty to think about the real needs of students at this point. Do they need an ivory tower or not? Dr. Wilson argues that they do.

M.R.

3

The Needs of Students

BRYAN WILSON

The needs of present-day students cannot be understood without some regard to the changing character of universities themselves, and the changing circumstance of young people in contemporary society. I shall try to look at these needs from these two perspectives. To say this is not to abandon the belief that there are certain abiding needs of youth, and some values which must persist both in the changing university and in a changing world. My own consideration of these matters has been informed by seven years spent as sub-warden, and later as warden, in a small hall of residence in a red-brick university. In this circumstance I was able to spend almost every term-time evening, and many evenings of vacation talking to—and listening to—students. I was able to maintain sustained relationships. I state this circumstance at the outset by way of presenting my credentials for the provocative discussion which follows. Some may consider my conclusions wrong, but I am not prepared to believe—on the strength of my particular experience—that they are wrong because I am misinformed about students. Their deeper needs are, today, paradoxically and despite—perhaps because of—the extraordinary concern with university expansion, society's need for technologists and the educational rat-race with other countries, the increasingly forgotten element in the educational situation.

THE FUNCTIONS OF A UNIVERSITY

The minimal functions of universities are the advancement and the transmission of knowledge. It is predominantly in terms of the need for greater dissemination of knowledge that the ex-

44

pansion of universities has recently been canvassed, on the assumption that our society needs a vastly increased proportion of knowledgeable people, who will help us to keep up with the Russians and the Americans in the maintenance of scientific advancement and the improvement of our living standards. The demands are mainly for the technologically educated, and one might suppose that the Russian Sputnik of 1957 appears to have been the beginning of the new wave of intensive pressure for university expansion. There are a variety of contestable value propositions in this argument for expansion, which must here be left aside. What is more to the point is the fact that university education, as we have traditionally known and valued it in our society, has always been very much more than the mere transmission of knowledge. In England the universities themselves have regarded their distinctive mission as the dissemination of human, liberal, civilizing values. They have sought to introduce students to the richness of our cultural inheritance, to provide access to the cumulative aesthetic, literary, philosophic and scientific resources of mankind, and to stimulate intellectual discussion and critical assessment in a context in which young people have leisure and opportunity to savour all the best that our culture has to offer. Thus information alone has never been the concern of English universities—it has been merely the basis on which an educated understanding and a cultivated attitude could be developed.

The ideal has, of course, often outstripped the reality, but the ideal has been there, and has in itself, even if only as a myth (and often as myth with a good deal of substance) been of importance to the activities and ethos of the universities. It would still find widespread assent among academics, as a formulation of the business with which they are engaged: nowadays there would, undoubtedly be dissenting voices to maintain that universities were properly concerned only with the transmission of specific skills and specific know-how. The voices are those of the new professional men of the academic world, whose interests are often confined to their own subject, who despise the wider cultural concerns which still persist in universities, and who describe them in pejorative terms as 'frills' or 'goodies'. The expression of the ideal is, however, to be found heavily emphasized in the speeches of vice-chancellors—more fully by the older scholarly type of vice-chancellor, perhaps less so by the more modern money-raising vice-chancellor, who sees his role more as a conductor of public relations rather than as a custodian of scholarly values. But the ideal may also be found in the charters of universities, and in the activities which universities sponsor, such as, exhibitions, concerts, lectures, demonstrations. It is still true to say that these activities are sponsored primarily for their own sake, and have not yet been reduced to mere goodwill gestures towards a public from whom donations, grants and contributions from the rates are being actively sought. There is, then, a body of easily available evidence about the values which have been built into the functions of British universities.

My concern is with the university in this role as an agency of intellectual and cultural transmission and dissemination. I leave aside its functions as a research institution. My premise is that as an educative agency the university is an organization with certain distinctive value-commitments, its primary responsibility being to produce the educated man in the wide sense of the word. That universities embody certain distinct values is evidenced by their welfare orientation, and in their widely manifested concern for students. Education operates on the assumption that there are certain objective values which older and more experienced persons can transmit to younger and less experienced ones in a university context. The tutorial system and the residential arrangements of our universities are an example of this welfare orientation which amounts to more than merely providing lodging houses, health facilities and refectories. It is 'welfare' in terms of the cultural and intellectual well-being of the student, who is being introduced to the traditionally highly valued aspects of our civilization. He is being given the opportunity to grow into another kind of person, and not merely to pick up notions which he can regurgitate at examination time. This, at least, is the assumption of the types of provision which universities make.

PRESENT THREATS TO UNIVERSITY VALUES

In course of time all institutions tend to suffer an attenuation of function and a dilution of values. Commitment may diminish, especially as there is compromise between original intentions and subsequent pressures, both internal and external. New purposes are added and old ones are (often involuntarily) surrendered or relaxed. High officials become preoccupied with the merely mechanical operation of the institution, particularly in periods of expansion, and lose sight of the values which institutions are supposed to embody. New disciplines, with very different requirements and different demands, are accepted, and these have consequences for the whole institution, for the conception of the institution which is held in the minds of personnel and clientele alike. Whenever new functions or new purposes are grafted on to an organization which was not designed for them, this dilution of value commitment, or confusion of goals, must occur. Under pressure to expand, the universities become especially vulnerable to threats to their values. A number of such threats might be listed:

1. There tends to occur distinct competition between institutions. This is likely to be particularly acute when they are seeking to establish what is nowadays called 'an image' and what used to be called a reputation. (An image is a surface presentation intended to elicit favourable responses, whether these are justified by the actual reality or not; a reputation was related to the actual and enduring characteristics of an institution, not merely to its façade.) Obviously new institutions cannot enjoy a reputation immediately, so they tend, especially in a society in which publicity values dominate over reality values, to succumb to the temptation to project an image as a substitute for building a reputation. The tendency of new universities to find a gimmick, and to 'put themselves over' with every device of publicity seeking, is especially evident. The search for publicity and the concentration on public relations illustrates the extent of the underlying competition between university institutions. Publicity is clearly a significant deflection of the purposes of a university. In terms of the received values of university education, a university in the news ought to be an object of suspicion.

Competition is also evident in other aspects of university development. The struggle for finance from the University Grants Committee is a struggle between universities and between departments within them. Universities also struggle not only to expand but also to avoid contraction when certain specialized departments exist in too many institutions and when greater concentration is demanded (as in the case of departments of Mining in the recent past). There is competition between departments in terms of the take-over of ancillary departments. Professorial imperialism is a common phenomenon of academic life, as professors seek to increase their students, staff, equipment and living space in a way which is not uncommon in the business world. But in the case of business such aggression is at least consonant with the ethics of economic activity; in universities it is a form of aggrandizement alien to the values of scholarship and of culture.

2. Institutional values have suffered dilution in the growth within universities of new types of discipline, particularly of applied disciplines, from business management to fuel technology. That these subjects should be taught somewhere is not in dispute; the only point at issue is that their introduction into universities has had consequences for these institutions themselves, altering them in unintended, unforeseen, and—in terms of commitments to their primary values—undesirable ways. These subjects are more instrumental, more confined to set skills, with less use for initiative, judgment and argument, than the traditional subjects. Learning in these disciplines is less a matter of reading, essay-writing, tutorial work and discussion, and more a matter of work done in drawing offices and laboratories. Thus, when away from the university and its nine-to-five curriculum, students in these subjects have very much less to do. In vacations they are not expected to read but rather to take jobs which are useful, and which are sometimes obligatory for their courses.[1] These time-dispositions differ radically from those of the arts, pure sciences and social sciences, and yet the existence of students with this type of timetable has an impact upon the rest. The technologies have affected ideas about study among students in other faculties, who would also like to be free in the evenings and to earn money in the vacations. These others also tend to develop a more instrumental attitude to their studies (not only as a consequence of this association with technologists, although this is one factor at work). Increasingly they, too, see the university as training them in specific skills—however inappropriate this approach is to their subject.

3. A third circumstance of institutional vulnerability is in the change of personnel. As universities grow, so there must be an

induction of staff who would not previously have been appointed. Narrower criteria of selection are likely to be applied, and the specialist who is not interested in learning and culture outside his own field, grows more common. The intensification of specialization itself promotes this result, unless deliberate steps are taken to mitigate the consequences. The attitude to academic life becomes more highly professionalized—teaching becomes just a job, in which commitment is to be defined and delimited. Lucky Jim becomes a reality, and narrow specialization sometimes appears to result in anti-intellectualism. Such personnel are more difficult to socialize to the values of particular institutions. They take the institutional framework for granted and accept and intensify its impersonality by their own professional responses to it. They do not see that their loyalties need be engaged towards the university itself. With the increase in number of this new type of academic man it is not easy to see how the values of the university community can escape dilution. As universities expand so the staff grows more mobile, becoming a migratory *élite*, sinking no roots in the life of the community but only in the profession which offers them advancement and career-opportunities.

4. The clientele obviously affects an institution. Today there is an alien youth culture which plays on the university through young people who are not primarily committed to the ideals of education. In some measure the youth culture draws its values from the entertainment industry. 'Work' becomes a bore, to be got through, and there is often resentment against lecturing which does not seem to be specifically useful for examination purposes. The pressure of the clientele can be made very evident even in the actual lecturing situation—by passive resistance to discussion of the wider implications of particular points (regarded as 'waffle') or even by extensive noises off and interruptions of lectures when dissatisfaction is more acute. Once the lecturer leaves the strictly 'examinable' items, particularly in the more factual subjects, he is often exposed to very emphatic pressure by his clientele, which can even lead to complete disruption of a lecture, especially at the beginning of sessions. All this reflects two characteristics of the clientele: the demand for a qualification and the demand for a good time. The qualification is the passport to a better job, to be gained without neces-

sarily becoming committed to a subject and without acquiring a more cultivated mind. Mechanical processing, and a certificate of exposure to it, are what are demanded. Because education can be reduced to the time spent in lectures and labs., with intense 'swotting' in the weeks prior to examinations, there is plenty of time for the 'fun ethic' of contemporary society to be brought into the university, the permissive atmosphere of which has no defence against such importations. There is sometimes hooliganism, damage and injury.[2]

5. The public—as a clientele at one remove—also imposes pressures on the university in a variety of ways. The anxieties which a few years ago, were induced largely by the press about the selection system at 11+, have now shifted to anxieties about social selection at 18+, with the inevitable accompanying demand for a wider distribution of success. The public at large is unconcerned with the maintenance of standards and the intrinsic quality of educational and university experience: it is interested in the distribution of prestige, pay and access to better jobs. Status inflation, in a society in which rapid social mobility is possible and expectable, and for which demand grows, is not unlike monetary inflation: the end result is the devaluation of the commodity concerned, prestige and academic standards in the one case and specie in the other. The intrinsic quality of education is affected (and later its social evaluation) just as currency is affected in monetary inflation—a consequence of the over-distribution of a commodity the supply of which is easily increased on paper but the value of which rests on some much less easily expendable reality. The search for status in our society successively devalues particular status symbols. The birthright B.A., if ever we succumb to the demand, will obviously be of no use as a claim to status, as a criterion of income distribution, or as an objective assessment of ability or academic achievement. Nor, for other reasons, will it be an evidence of all-round education. The supply of a commodity which is scarce (perhaps because of limitations of ability, and certainly because we do not have the means to increase the supply whilst maintaining its character) and which is socially valued less for its intrinsic content than for its instrumental use and for the status which scarcity itself provides, cannot be increased without destroying both the extrinsic basis of its value and its intrin-

The Needs of Students

sic character. But in a democratic market-society these demands are hard to withstand: inflation and devaluation are the Achilles' heel of democratic systems and the pressure of demand falls on the quality of the commodity. Yet, as has been remarked, inflation is a disease which is enjoyed—in the short run—by its victims. Universities, as public institutions, are sensitive to criticism, sensitive about their 'image', and feel this, perhaps, more acutely in the short run than they feel the longer-run consequences of succumbing to demand. Freedom of action becomes difficult in this circumstance and the unpopular commitment to the maintenance of values and standards surrenders to the demand for increased distribution.

The consequences of pressures of this kind—and doubtless there are others—is uncertainty of purpose and conflict of values within universities. Expansion is apparently the easy and popular solution of all contemporary difficulties: values alone suffer. Expansion has an appeal because it offers improvement of personal circumstances to almost everyone. Some academics are attracted by the prospects of new posts as universities expand; the A.U.T. sees higher salaries and the increase of membership; vice-chancellors see growth of the enterprise with which they are identified; the public sees more opportunities for their children; and the political parties rejoice in an easy electoral gambit, distribute the new political largesse, and bid up the number of new universities at the rate of a public auction. One contemporary evidence of failure of nerve in the universities is the new willingness of university authorities to respond to the demands of its clientele—as if the academics themselves were no longer certain of the appropriate content and methods of education. Students have never been listened to as much as they are today, but the use of elaborate questionnaires and market research techniques may be little more than a publicity gimmick for universities which feel the need to demonstrate their 'progressive' approach. There is no reason to oppose consultation with students where their interests are affected—but it must be a sustained and natural process, reflecting joint concerns, and in the context of shared values; it must itself be an educative process, and the commitment to the educative ideals of universities must be an unchallengeable first premise. It is, in the curious condition of modern large universities, easier to 'buy students off' with a survey than to establish human relationships in which teacher and administrators *really* talk to students in a continuing discourse. Questionnaires have all the appeal of democratic measures. But they canvass opinions out of contexts, and simplify the complexities of the issues at stake. They often illustrate the prejudices of the investigators, but do so in a concealed way, and they respond to the limitations of their computers, missing the richness and diversity of the texture of real-life relationships. It is particularly alarming to find the results of this type of inquiry seriously regarded as the basis for the formulation of policy, when the research techniques which produce such results are open to such misuse.[3]

What one must ask is whether there are no implicit values within university education which can provide the basis for consultation and for decision-making? Ought these not to be changed, when necessary, as a result of deliberate decision, not as the unforeseen consequence of fashionable but dubious 'fact-finding' procedures? The problem is particularly acute in periods of expansion, when universities are threatened not only with the attenuation of values by internal adjustment to mass-education, but also by the reduced commitment of a less fully socialized clientele.

The conception of the university which I am propounding is both expensive and selective—not for the sake of expense and exclusiveness as such, but because these conditions appear to be necessary for the maintenance of the educational values of universities as we have known them. These values in themselves have not been disapproved of, or there would be no demand for the expansion of university education; instead, there would be a demand for education of a distinctly different sort. But only a minority can profit from what a university can do—not because only a few have the intellect (a matter still open to dispute) but because the system cannot operate at the mass level and because few develop a genuine commitment to this educative experience. Its expansion will merely over-extend its resources, destroying its value for all. Despite the popular pressure for university entrance relatively few are prepared for the intellectual commitment which it demands. The present pressure is not a sudden conversion of the population to a taste for scholarship but only a demand by parents, and in some measure by students, for

access to job opportunities and—for some would-be students—
a desire to experience the permissiveness of the university life.
Expansion, because of the mass clientele which it implies, will
make more difficult the task of winning the commitment of
young people to the university's mission. Furthermore, increase
of numbers as such threatens the contexts in which this educational experience can be created. It is an education which, to
be of maximum value to those who receive it, and to the society
which will enjoy the influence of those who receive it, should
be intensified rather than extended. Expansion jeopardizes university values, and in doing so it reduces the value of university
education to students and to society. It thus creates an elaborate
deception of the public.

OLD EXPECTATIONS AND NEW RESPONSES OF STUDENTS

This is the background against which we have to see the
student experience at the present time. They often arrive at
university with two distinct and contradictory, indeed un-
related, sets of assumptions. In the first place they expect an
elevated intellectual atmosphere and look forward to a mysteri-
ous experience which will result in intellectual transformation:
they expect to emerge with new power. They are vague about
how such transformation will be accomplished and tempera-
mentally ill-disposed to the idea of its imperceptible gradual-
ness. They have little idea of what might be entailed in the
process, but there is a vague hope of increased articulateness
and heightened understanding. It is a set of assumptions to
which disillusionment is an almost necessary consequence; unless, from the outset, someone with time and sympathy is prepared to give this aspiration realistic dimensions, the strength
of this pristine aspiration will never be harnessed. The mere
experience of university routine will otherwise be enough to
destroy it. The other assumptions are those of the youth culture
—that the university is the confrontation with an alien and
somewhat suspect world, that it threatens the individual's tastes,
attitudes, life-habits and values, and that this threat is to be
resisted.

Clearly these assumptions do not have this degree of pre-
cision and articulateness in the minds of those students who hold
them. They are not conscious responses. They appear to be

53

more clearly manifested in those whose subjects of study allow them to think in terms of a set of skills to be impersonally acquired and carried off—without the need even to breathe the atmosphere of the place in which learning has to take place. At their worst, they represent a refusal to grow up or to surrender the advantages of being young, and in particular a refusal to be educated. The desire to be transformed without having to undergo the suffering of change implies a resistance to academic commitment: the personality remains free of obligations, and the university experience is detached and impersonal—as compartmentalized as are the activities of work in contemporary society. There is little conception of the need for an investment of the self in the process: university obligations are a routine, to be kept at a minimum. To get away with a good result without actually having to be involved in the process of learning is more important than to understand or to be educated. There is a widespread mistrust of intellectuality and contempt for those who cultivate the intellect or devote themselves to cultural concerns. The union newspaper knew the situation well, when in its well-meaning way it directed an editorial to freshmen, and told them that 'Culture is not really a dirty word'.[4]

Disenchantment with the university is by no means an uncommon experience for students. There is the deadening routine of mass institutions; the queues, the inevitable overcrowding; the extensive petty pilfering.[5] Refectories are frequestly more reminiscent of London street-corner cafeterias—but less clean, less efficient and often offering less attractive fare. The lavatories are liberally decorated with *graffiti* which would be quite in tone with down-town public conveniences. The quickly deteriorating furniture of common rooms and lounges, sometimes speeded on its way by deliberate acts of vandalism, is over-used and completes the depersonalized, institutional atmosphere. But in such institutional contexts young people have to live. It is not surprising that much of their behaviour reveals little sensitivity to others, when others are just part of the institutionalized mass. So one finds that essentially private types of behaviour are indulged in in very public places. Parents on casual visits are sometimes shocked to find so much 'snogging' in the public parts of union buildings and even of university buildings. Obviously no one finds it his business to interfere: and the much-prized 'university atmosphere' for some appears to stimulate neither self-discipline nor social constraints. Young people in the mass often appear to be out of touch with the established values of the universities they populate.

In the mass university, too, there appears to be a heightening of *Us-Them* responses. The bigger universities are, the more likely it is that two cultures develop—not Snow's two cultures of arts and sciences, but the more tragic separation of staff and students. Students increasingly associate only with students; from them they acquire their categories of norms and values for interpreting their social situation. The facile dichotomy *Us-Them*, helps students to regulate their responses to a strange new world. It provides ready-made stereotypes of behaviour, and it is buttressed by all the paraphernalia of the contemporary youth culture. The *hip* and *square* categories, the generational lines of cleavage which they imply, are readily applied in the university context—and more especially since intellectualism, civilized values, good manners and cultural concerns are precisely the hall-marks of the stuffy fuddy-duddies as the entertainment leaders of the youth culture depict them. It is probably only a minority of students for whom these categories have firm meaning and who are not at times ambivalent in their responses, but the pervasiveness of the youth culture tends to define and structure social situations for young people in these terms. The extent of the *Us-Them* response is the extent to which young people are insulated from the values of the university, into which the teaching staff is supposed to socialize them. In fact the young socialize themselves, drawing little from the university experience except as a specially permissive context of the youth culture. Apathy and loutishness, periodically condemned by the Union officials themselves, become widespread responses, while there is a strong belief that 'academics are not much interested in us'.

The *Us-Them* response is conditioned by ignorance—a complete absence of information about the nature of the university's mission, its wider concerns and its traditional values. Many students learn very little about the university to which they belong (indeed the very idea that they 'belong' sounds almost quaint). Except in the context of games, their loyalties to it are low. Universities characteristically lack channels of internal information. As they grow and diversify, so they become too many-sided for students to feel that they *know* the university, and can become committed to it. Yet often there is no effective smaller unit with which students can become strongly involved, except in some cases, the department. But departments are themselves often too specialized, too narrowly instrumental to take on the community functions which strengthen allegiances and summon loyalties. Some departmental heads—viewing their function in professional, intellectual terms—prefer to maintain a certain impersonality within these units. Finally, in the sense of the university's values and its mission to introduce young people to a wider intellectual culture, the department is ill-suited to be the sole unit of identification for the student. Nor do all students respond very readily to the idea of committing themselves to the university or its mission. Increasingly used to the impersonal character of institutions from their now enlarged or comprehensive schools, they reach a point where they merely use the facilities rather than become involved in an intellectual community. Often they do not want the university to impinge much upon them. They are not realistically prepared for any challenge to the values they have brought with them, nor for any inducement to develop a critical faculty towards them. Often when the first millennial dream of transformation is over, they settle for a mechanical relation to their studies and disengagement with everything else for which the university exists.

As the disillusionment with the prospect of painless transformation grows, and as university life is increasingly revealed as merely a shoddy extension of life-patterns learned before, in a context where (compared with school and home) people care less about you, so the trumpeted claims for the university (by Vice-Chancellors at Freshers' Conferences, for instance) grow more hollow, and the inarticulate disinclination to commit oneself to academic pursuits, beyond the strictly necessary and the mechanically routine, grows stronger. Disillusionment is frequently expressed—about the crowded time-tables; the dreary routine lectures with blackboards covered with formulae; the impersonality of relationships with academics, and the fact that students never meet lecturers outside the classroom, or when they do, the lecturers do not acknowledge them. Obviously this process does not occur in all cases, but it appears to be of widespread incidence in red-brick universities.[6] Some students meet inspiring tutors; some come with higher commitment from their schools, if they have been lucky enough to have had sustained contact with a master who has transmitted values and enthusiasm to them; some discover really absorbing things in their subjects (but how many others discover that what they thought would be fascinating turns out to be drudgery?). Where inspiration is derived from the university context, it appears to be derived from personal contact—a type of contact which grows less common, and is less sustained, as universities grow bigger. One must, of course, be aware that those who later complain that they never meet lecturers outside the classroom, may not display much enthusiasm to do so, nor show much civilized receptivity to such encounters when they do occur. But this in itself merely illustrates the role which academics must play in regard to students. They must recognize both the complaint and the causes of the diffidence which make it all the easier for complaint to occur. It is they who must break into the cycle of disillusionment-frustration-criticism-diffidence. This paradoxical situation corresponds to the desire for transformation whilst yet retaining one's personality and values unscathed in the university encounter.

It is for the university to recognize this reluctance on the part of its clientele and therefore the need to be more active in the socialization of students. The university must provide a total environment in which intellectual interests, regard for cultural achievement, liberal values and critical discernment are a natural context for the student. The business of civilizing is to make what are regarded as 'artificial' circumstances (the charge which students often make against universities) into natural circumstances. The university must carry this concern well beyond the lecture-room, and this, indeed, is the only justification for universities setting up as lodging-house keepers. The need is not to provide places for students to live in, but to provide places in which young people are educated and acquire university values. It may be that over-lecturing (and many academics complain that their students are over-lectured) is a half-conscious acknowledgment in red-brick universities that the university must provide a more total context for students. The lecture-room is one of the few agencies which universities have discovered for the stimulation of the intellect and the transmission of scholarly concerns. Since these universities offer little elsewhere, they attempt to deal with the general *malaise* of the university through the one procedure which is already well established, ill-adapted as it is to treatment of the disease.

But, in general, universities do not give much heed to the lack of commitment in many of their students. Indeed, they operate on entirely contrary assumptions—the assumption of a self-disciplined, committed clientele, which, given a high degree of freedom, will avail itself of the intellectual and cultural facilities provided. These assumptions are evident in the permissive atmosphere of universities and it might be argued that they are assumptions necessary to education itself. But students do not—in the main—arrive at university prepared for the rigours of an academic involvement to which they are completely dedicated. For many of them university is simply what follows from success in school—it is a prize in terms of a freer atmosphere, independence, a good time, and a necessary processing towards the attainment of a better job. Academic motivation has, for most, little part in it, yet it is exactly this which the university in conducting its operations assumes to be present. It assumes intellectual and scholarly self-discipline—two qualities against which the contemporary youth culture militates most trenchantly, even if they had been acquired in any measure in school. But although there is little reason to suppose that undergraduates possess these qualities at the outset, the university does little to inculcate them. When lecturers find that students are not highly committed they often shrug their shoulders and disclaim responsibility. One has heard them say such things as, 'Oh well, if they haven't sense to give their minds to it, its their own funeral'; 'If they don't want to work, they shouldn't be here'.

But shouldn't they? The argument is one scarcely considered by the Robbins Committee, but that committee was hardly concerned with the education of the individual. These responses by academics are, of course, a divestment of moral responsibility just at the point at which their obligations to students are most vital. In the present situation, the responsibility of academics is not only to teach students, but also to induce them to want to be taught. (But the very word *taught* takes on an archaic ring—since many contemporary young people dislike the inequality implicit in the idea—they do not mind discussing, even on the strength of brief acquaintance with the subject, but they are less patient about learning how to explore it.)

It is still vaguely assumed that scholarly values should be inhaled from the atmosphere of universities. But the atmosphere has changed: the clientele itself has radically affected it. In the past it seems that people brought with them to the university values which were much less dissonant with the university's business than is now the case. At the time adult society was *still* respected, and the accumulated knowledge of society was esteemed, so that those who entered universities, even if not always desperately keen to learn themselves, were not root-and-branch opposed to what learning stood for. There was not then a generational sub-culture, promoted by mass media, with values largely alien to those of the academic and cultural tradition of our society. The universities had less need to concern themselves with socializing their intake, with transmitting an appreciation of scholarly values to them. In addition, they could claim less responsibility than they can legitimately claim now. People came at their own or their fathers' expense more frequently and their education was seen as something for their own personal benefit, or as a personal accomplishment, in which society at large was not really involved, certainly not in the way in which society's supposed needs for university-educated people are now emphasized. Universities were not asked, as they now are, by grant-awarding authorities, to give details of the progress of particular students in receipt of public money. In the welfare state the universities have—or should have—new responsibilities, not the least of which is that of ensuring that they have done everything possible to win the commitment of their increased clientele to the educative process in which they are to be jointly involved. But as numbers have increased and deficiency of commitment has become more pronounced, so the tutorial system, which is perhaps the best systematic method of winning this academic response from students, has been placed under greater strain. It often exists more fully on paper than in reality, for the satisfaction of vice-chancellors and others sufficiently 'far-up' the hierarchy to know relatively little of the grass-roots experience of the students. In universities, no less than in other institutions, information is corrupted as it goes upwards, as successive ranks of the hierarchy justify themselves in their reports, and rationalize and formalize 'available information'.

Bryan Wilson

The failure of the universities to evolve an appropriate process of socializing students has been all the more accentuated because the prevailing social and cultural context supports university values less than it used to do. To say this, at a time when pressure to get in to universities has been so much increased, and when universities make daily headlines for the press and television, may seem paradoxical, but it is precisely this popularization which threatens the universities most. Their mission proceeds best when it proceeds quietly—its real concerns are not news or newsworthy, and the consciousness of newsability is itself a corruption of their purposes. But today universities are reliant on a public which is less informed about them and their role in society and less committed to the maintenance of their distinctive values. This is expressed, at the simplest level, in the failure of parents to appreciate the need for young people living at home to do academic work in the evenings and in the vacations; in the general public's mistrust of the permissiveness of university life, especially when students flaunt their leisure on sunny days and appear not to work. (This mistrust, interestingly, now gains more substance as permissiveness is misused and scholarly commitment declines.) The very popularity of universities jeopardizes their character, and the persistence of their endeavour. But the character of the wider society has altered in other ways, ways which particularly affect the clientele which the universities recruit. They are now more alienated from the values espoused by universities than ever before.

THE PERVASIVE YOUTH CULTURE

In contemporary society young people live in a much more segregated generational context than they did. No doubt youth has always, and appropriately, expressed its rebellion, but it has never before existed in a circumstance where the gestures of rebelliousness have been manufactured for the young as they now are. Mass communication and mass production have made possible the dissemination of what might be termed expressive postures and expressive products. These products are highly profitable to their producers and distributors, but we are still quite unaware of their 'social costs'. Today we have an industry concerned with the canalization and manipulation of youthful

60

rebelliousness, which it succeeds in transforming into delinquescent, anti-intellectual defiance. Prospective undergraduates are as involved as consumers in this market as are most other youngsters—intelligence alone is no protection against compulsive generational behaviour which is, on the one hand, astutely exploited, and on the other, insufficiently inhibited by older generations. Had distinctive class patterns of behaviour prevailed among young people, middle-class youngsters would have been insulated from the growing conformity of the youth culture by the class values learned in their homes and schools. Generational segregation, the enormous increase in real income among young people (earned or given as pocket-money), the replacement of parental and scholastic values and tastes by those of more aggressive and less disinterested agencies—all this has meant the increasing conformity of styles and values within all classes of the younger generation. In this situation education—necessarily transmitted from older generations—appears to have less and less to do with attitudes, tastes, standards and morals, and to be reduced to skills which leave unaffected the character of the individual who has acquired them.

The present youth culture does more than give organized expression to what might be classed as 'natural' youthful rebellion. The postures of the youth culture constitute a generational defence-mechanism against the charge of failure in a society which places a high premium on educational success. The response is that 'we never accepted success in those terms, anyhow'. But the rationalization for failure, which the vast majority need in some form or another, is accepted as a cultural mode, even by those who succeed—or who are succeeding—partly as an insurance against future failure, but also because in the youth culture this type of success has been devalued, and other sub-cultural goals have been substituted. An alternative reference group has been established: instead of parents, teachers, elders and mentors, there are contemporaries, and their judgment matters more, since more of life is lived with them. It is nothing new for young people to debunk the values of their elders, but the process of debunking appears to be more serious and systematic; it has been transformed into ready-made attitudes and commodities which the young individual *must* possess. Those who exploit this market—journalists, entertainers, manufacturers—naturally go on record as being liberal, progressive

61

Bryan Wilson

and on the side of youth (as if teachers and parents were in some curious way always against youth). Their concern is not for the young people—who will one day be not-so-young—but is a form of social discrimination in which generational divisions have merely replaced class or racial divisions.

All of this means that students today are very much less differentiated from young people outside the universities than they used to be, and that many bring these manufactured generational values with them into the universities. Although at an idealized level these youngsters are motivated to come to university by the prospect of obtaining social power and income through education, the university also has an appeal as a permissive context in which a good time can be had. The culture in which these young people participate is not only different, but also hostile to the values of the universities, and thus, because of their permissive atmosphere, the universities are themselves vulnerable. The heroes of this youth culture illustrate this point. These heroes are socially mobile 'stars' of the entertainment world, and their accomplishments are often imitated at the cost of considerable effort. Their social mobility has not depended on training, intellect, civilized values or liberal education (nor, be it noted, on competitive examination). Indeed, these would be positive hindrances to the 'discovery' of those native talents from which success springs. (There is at least one celebrated case of a 'student' who gave up his studies for the prospects of stardom in the entertainment world.) Success in this case owes nothing to what the star has been able to make his own of the accumulated cultural tradition, and not much even to hard work.

But rapid and glamorous achievement are the very antithesis of success in the university, where close acquaintance with accumulated knowledge and its development are vital to proving one's competence. The myth of easy, overnight, untutored success is part of the entertainment ideology of the youth culture—and it is success which can be intimately appreciated by a very wide audience, the whole generational reference group. Academic success is hazardous; subject to frequent hurdles, each of which is the preparation for a higher one to follow, and with an audience which, in terms of intelligent appreciation, grows ever smaller and less easily impressed. And it is all hard work, all the way. Nourished on the values of the youth culture, there is less willingness to postpone present gratificat'ons for future benefits than once there was. Marriage is earlier, and, egged on by the mass media and by some academics, sexual experience is earlier still. University education assumes the self-discipline of its students as a necessary concomitant of the permissive atmosphere it provides; it assumes willing postponements of alternative activities and ends. Marriage, money and the pleasures which money can buy, and time-taking pursuits such as motoring (and motor-making) are ill-adapted to the university context. But for those brought up in the contemporary youth culture the demands of the university, and the circumstance of learning are in themselves acute threats to pleasure. Learning imposes a sense of deprivation. It means, if the rules are followed, less money, less time for pleasure and less opportunity for extensive social contact. Study is largely sedentary and solitary, but the youth culture is active and gregarious. The social pressures on young people, from which we do so little to insulate our students, make it more difficult for them to sacrifice time, money and pleasure for the sake of cultural and intellectual enrichment—two commodities rapidly losing value, and no longer regarded as rewards in themselves. The demand for fun and money is such that one has met students who wanted to rearrange the times of graduate seminars so that dances might be more easily attended, and others who, though in receipt of a full grant, have surreptitiously undertaken paid employment in term-time, or less surreptitiously when the paid employment has been with a dance band earning quite 'big money' several nights a week.

The pressures of the youth culture make the retention of scholarly values more difficult even among those who are more committed to them. Gresham's law operates, and more comes to mean worse—not necessarily because of the lower intellectual quality of students, but because the universities have devised no way of protecting their values in the face of a large new unsocialized clientele. The permissive context itself militates against 'doing anything about it'. It is easier for academics, if they perceive these trends, to seek refuge and solace in their own work: moral responsibility is not readily accepted and in a situation where the rewards and prestige go for published work or for participation in university politics, or work on public committees, it is easier to disregard the wider implications and obligations of teaching, for which, no matter how well it is done, there is little recognition and small extrinsic reward. If the personnel can avoid the implications of this situation, the clientele clearly prefers a situation where it is less troubled, even if, from time to time it resents the lack of interest shown. There is a prevailing mood which favours non-interference in student affairs—'it's their life', it is said. But education is necessarily an interference, a moral commitment to the well-being of students; since education implies interference, re-structuring of orientations and values, the circumstances in which education takes place have also to be subject to interference. To use the word 'interference' is to accept the word of the *laissez-faire* theorists in universities; as 'help' and 'participation', 'interference' is an implicit necessity of the system.

THE NEED FOR THE IVORY TOWER

If I am right in my foregoing analysis, then it seems to me that universities, if they are to maintain their mission, must take radical steps to insulate young people from influences which not only distract them from education, but create conflicts about the values which they should accept. It is frequently asserted that the universities must not lose touch with 'real life'. Just what is meant by 'real life' is somewhat elusive. In an age of mass communication it is hard to see how knowledge of the main social activities, of political, social and educational debate, and the changing course of fashion, can be avoided, wherever one is. Frequently the argument is that halls of residence protect and cloister students too much, that there is something more vital in roughing it in digs. As a warden of a hall for some years I found it a curious idea in colleagues that they should believe that a landlady was more real or more relevant to students than I was. The argument sometimes had a curious class overtone— that working- and lower-middle-class life (and most digs were of this type) was more robust than that of other classes—an assumption which, true or false, merely reflected a preference. Whatever else, there was no doubt that the facilities of such digs did not participate deeply in the distinctive traditions of English universities. A great many of the students themselves were from these classes and needed no deepening of insight in these respects, but rather the enlargement of horizons which a more pervasive university atmosphere alone could provide. The 'real life' argument sometimes came from technologists, who found in it their counterpoise to academicism, and revealed in it their anxiety about some of the university traditions for which they felt themselves ill-adapted. Their demand for 'real life' as they chose to call it, was merely a further evidence of the pressures which these disciplines impose on the universities and which militate against distinctive academic traditions.

When the argument for the exposure of students to more 'real life' is used in support of the location of universities in cities, one can only suppose that it means that students should be exposed to the horrors of the motor transport situation and parking, and should go to town dances.[7] In fact our incoming freshmen have never been so worldly-wise as they now are, never so completely indoctrinated with the values of the wider society (and I do not exclude the ex-service generation in which I was a student). They have heard and seen and imbibed much more of the world's values. Only a few years ago students were much more favourably disposed to a whole complex of cultural values than they are now. A decade ago popular music was not nearly so much a part of student culture as it has now become. Students then were conscious of the expectations of others that they should aspire to things more consonant with university values. Partly as a consequence of the expansion of mass media with all the prestige of its curious techno-demagogic authority, the values of young people have considerably altered, and their readiness for the challenging context which a university at its best should provide, has diminished.

The university now has to begin a process of 'de-indoctrination' of young people before its own mission can be begun, since its clientele is probably more alienated from university values than any previous generation of students. It thus becomes vital for a university to extend and intensify its influence over its students and to create a pervasive atmosphere in which its own values are dominant, unequivocal and resistant to the values of the wider society. The extraordinary increase in the influence of commercial and entertainment values in our society has as yet met no positive response from the universities, except perhaps in the emergence of the television-don, doubtless single-mindedly seeking to raise the tone of public discussion. It is true, of course, that universities lack the apparent authority of

Bryan Wilson

the mass media, lack their technological slickness, their evident efficiency, conspicuous wealth, and capacity to create fashions. They cannot enter the public lists in a conflict over values. But ought they to accept the values of these media; ought they not to maintain a mission to transform by education, the wider society which the mass media now so dominate? To do this, the university must re-immerse students in precisely those ideals and values which in 'real life' have become, so often, sullied. The university needs to be a place apart, transmitting the values of academic integrity, sound scholarship and cultural achievement and, for all these things, winning the commitment of students. Its weapons in the struggle for the minds of students must be insulation from the wider society; the intensification of academic values in university life; the infusion of these values into every area of its activity, no matter how ancillary. There is no reason why the lodgings office, the bursar's department and the refectory should not be as fully imbued with humane, academic and cultural values as other branches of the university—and it is most vital that this should be so in halls of residence. Nor need the universities fear the response of the clientele, as they now so manifestly do in their pusillanimous temporizing on basic issues: if they can but grasp the millennialist dreams of the freshmen, their more positive confrontation is likely to be both understood and accepted by students themselves.

To make evident the nature of the precious shared commitments it is offering, the university needs to take these young worldlings out of the world a little and into the ivory tower. It must give them other ideals than those of the dubious jazz-musicians, the popular press, pop singers, TV commentators, women of easy virtue and the contemporary satirists, whose sayings and doings so dominate the mass media, and about whom youngsters know so much more than they know of philosophers and scientists. If the universities are to have an impact on the wider society it must be when their undergraduates *return* to it, after an adequate education, and after making clear to them the nature of the commitment which is implicit in their decision to become students. It means, of course, the acceptance by academics of much more work and personal concern for students, but if the universities can return people to the world who have acquired critical eyes, whose values are not automatically those of a conformist (sometimes, of course, conformingly non-con-

66

formist) mass culture, they will probably achieve more towards remaking our society than they will ever do if they confine their role to that of mere institutes of instruction.

EXPANSION AND 'BIG UNIVERSITIES' AS A THREAT TO EDUCATION

The student's experience of the university is threatened by two internal phenomena—departmentalization and expansion. The civic universities in particular tend to be structured as collections of departments—and all too often a student's total university experience is conditioned by this circumstance. His understanding of the wider concerns of the university is undeveloped, and his loyalties to those wider concerns is unengaged. Only the Union and the halls of residence mitigate this pattern of cleavage, and the Union tends now to be too big an organization to offer really good facilities of an educational kind to any except the tiny minority of the politically active. In large institutions dominant patterns of cleavage are not counteracted by centralization but rather by the establishment of alternative lines of subdivision, which create unity in diversity by the creation of many small cross-cutting associations.[8] Departmentalization is clearly a consequence of specialization, associated with increasing emphasis on learned skills, but its consequence tends to be that no department is much concerned with the maintenance of the more general values of the university as a whole. The results can be seen in one especially cogent example, though it has other applications: students often gain a narrow impression of their own subject, fail to see any connection between disciplines, are not introduced to wider questions, and take as a *natural order* of objective categories the breakdown of subjects into departmental concerns.[9]

Expansion will alter the nature of the university and will diminish what students can derive from it. Much has been made in the Robbins Report and elsewhere of the maintenance of the staff-student ratio. The elementary fallacy is recurrently committed of assuming that a ratio of 1 staff member to 8 students is the same thing in an institution of 10,000 as it is in an institution of 1,000. In fact little is so irrelevant to the texture of social relationships as this artificial ratio: the total number is more significant in determining the atmosphere of an institution. The ratio is a typical piece of quantitative misinformation about the qualitative. When staff reach a certain number they form a society of their own, self-sufficient and gaining all they need for social and intellectual intercourse from among themselves. They have less impact on students, and two sub-cultures develop within a collectivity in which the interests of the two groups stand in ever less clearly understood relation to each other. Among a hundred staff and a thousand students there is a possibility that everyone can know everyone else—the contours of the community at least can be discerned. But when staff number five hundred, it is likely to be the experience of each individual that he actually knows *fewer* people even among the staff. Many surface contacts replace a smaller number of more significant associations. The university acquires an impersonal atmosphere, men become anonymous to each other, and this circumstance dictates social relationships. Communication —the vital business of universities—is reduced, information is increasingly confined to the instrumental, the sense of shared participation in a meaningful enterprise disappears, sometimes for academics as well as for students. The ideal of the impact of mind on mind is surrendered, occurring only randomly here and there. The basis of confidence of students in staff, and respect of staff for students, diminishes. The academic increasinly finds himself 'doing a job' for a university which increasingly expresses its regard for him in strictly material terms, communicated through bureaucratic administrative procedures. As the university grows in size, he is less involved in its decision making, less committed to it as an investment of personal goodwill; the manifestation of goodwill may, indeed, be regarded by the more completely bureaucratized as eccentric behaviour. As the two sections of the university live in increasingly impersonal relationship—which I have underscored by calling them 'personnel' and 'clientele'—so the academic absolves himself from moral responsibility for students. They cease in the strict sense to be regarded as persons with personal claims. For some this circumstance permits judgments that 'what is wrong with this place is the type of students we get'—without much commitment to doing anything about altering that type.

Yet the current advocacy of bigger universities goes virtually unchallenged.[10] Bigger is assumed to mean better. The case of larger universities appears to rest on a vari ety of rather curious associations.[11] Bigger universities, it is said, alone justify the expense of cyclotrons and computers and other expensive scientific equipment. The argument might have force if universities were profit-making organizations, dependent on mass sales to justify technical innovations, but since universities are so overwhelmingly supported by state funds, either as direct grants or through the fossilized remnant of an earlier system, as student fees, the connection is meaningless. The state could supply equipment for selected institutions, which could be of any size. Since undergraduates do not work at the frontiers of research, the relevance of their number to the provision of expensive equipment is hard to understand. It is hard to see why a university has to have 1,500 or 2,000 arts and social science students before the physics department merits consideration for the provision of special facilities for its two or three score graduate research students.

It is said that a big American university offers a greater diversity of subjects and teachers. This is in itself true, but what is the significance of this point? How specialized do we wish undergraduate education to be: how many divisions of subjects are necessary to equip young people of this age, and in what degree of refinement? The supermarket approach to studies appears to have little to commend it, except to allow undergraduates to seek 'soft options' and bizarre combinations without anywhere acquiring anything basic. Our own recent developments, fortunately, see the need for broadening the range of student experience rather than for multiplying the courses of narrow specialization. One might doubt whether many specialized fields were particularly suitable for undergraduate study. If this is so, size merely means larger numbers of people doing rather similar courses—and in this circumstance size becomes a disadvantage on other grounds. Graduate students, who may need specialized supervision, can always move to institutions where this is available. Students rarely get a choice of teachers, except by choosing specialized courses, where this is allowed, and this is choice of course rather than of teacher. On the other hand, in small universities students often get the benefit of informal association with tutors and lecturers—which amounts *in effect* to a larger range of association with academics than they are likely to experience in the mass institution.

The other assumptions about big universities are of a similar type. It is argued that in a larger institution there are more people with whom scholars can discuss their work. But this assumes very much more academic discussion than can ever in fact take place. It would be interesting to know in just how much distinctly technical discussion academics actually engage with each other: in most fields the number of people with whom such discussion is possible outside one's immediate department (and sometimes even within it) is probably relatively few. Cross-disciplinary fertilization is a fairly rare phenomenon, and it seems doubtful whether big universities would really very much facilitate its increase. Specialization in most fields means that scholars must seek out those with whom they can profitably discuss their research. In a small island with (still) reasonable public transport facilities, frequent conferences, visiting lectureships and seminars which often bring scholars from different universities together, there seems little case for the establishment of larger universities on these grounds. Associated with this argument is frequently one which suggests that undergraduates also benefit from the more extensive mixing with students of more diversified backgrounds and of different nationalities. The argument may have some relevance to the smaller type of American state college with largely local intake. It is hard to believe that it has the same relevance in England, where in even the smallest universities there are radically diverse social types. The argument is naïve about the nature of social contacts, and the number of meaningful social relationships which the individual can sustain. It seems altogether likely that people of other nations are better known, and better cared for, in a community of a thousand, than in a community of ten thousand, where they are likely to form national or regional cliques. If a university is large enough to provide people with an interesting choice of friends, from a community the periphery of which can be known, so that choice at least has meaning, then the optimum position from this point of view has been reached. Increase of size beyond this simply implies greater superficiality of most relationships and ultimately the absence of any relationship with the vast majority of one's fellows. Those who will be rejected are those of divergent social, racial or national type, since the basis of relationships in this impersonal context will most probably be on the basis of initial similarities of values and background. Big universities impede effective social mixing.

The Needs of Students

The advocates of large universities tend to see the problems associated with them in administrative terms—they are, after all, universities in which the administration is likely to grow in power and in influencing the atmosphere of the institution. The problems they acknowledge are those of congestion, over-crowding, rebuilding and parking space. Unfortunately they tend also to assume that once they have solved these problems they have solved all problems, and that by providing good material facilities they have administered into being a university. Those problems which cannot be administratively defined, such as the maintenance of a texture of relationships, are, for the administrators, non-problems. They have been eliminated by a restatement of the university's business, by the surrender of its distinctive values. The university has been made over on the model of the business corporation. Like the business corporation profit and loss are calculated in essentially money terms—even in educational institutions, the idea that *educational* losses (as distinct from financial losses) should be entered in the ledger becomes a curiously alien thought. This, however, is the un-counted social cost of the so-called economics of scale.

One has seen some of the consequences of growth even in our own civic universities: students who, being unidentified within the university, fail to identify themselves with it; professors who have to be introduced to their own students, when, after three years in the same department, they chance to be brought to-gether for some social occasion; halls of residence in which in-vited guests become an embarrassment to students who do not want to entertain them and 'slope off' as soon as possible. Of course in these universities there are professors who pride them-selves on knowing all their students. But some manage to know them only by a twice-a-year handshake and a cheery word, expressing in this gesture their touching faith in human contact in the university. There are others who specialize in concern about student problems, but who never really meet their stu-dents till a problem arises, and who imagine that a problem can be dealt with independent of knowledge of the man whose problem it is. This is perhaps a common fallacy about the value of mental health facilities in universities, too. Mental health provision is itself merely a symptom of the sickness of the uni-versities, of the loss of genuine human contact between aca-demics and students.

71

Bryan Wilson

The weakest argument for the big universities is that if one is lecturing (soon it will be 'if a teaching machine is lecturing') to 20 students one may as well lecture to 500, and that thereby a tremendous saving is achieved in *per capita* costs. But this argument assumes that mere exposure to information is what constitutes university education. It assumes that size can be determined by the economics of exposure. The good teacher knows that 'what can be said' is much less significant educationally than 'what the student can make his own'. Slowly we move to a position in which routinized, impersonal exposure, without human contact, will provide students with the knowledge ('the notes') of which they should be in temporary possession in order to pass examinations. It has nothing to do with the tenor of their lives, it is unassociated with the spirit of inquiry, critical discrimination, broad cultural perspectives, unless these are derived from somewhere else. But if the universities are not to provide these things, where shall they be provided for the student? Where, indeed will they be maintained in the kind of society we are going to get?

Already in the older red-brick universities the routinization has advanced a long way. It is not uncommon for students to regard the material provided in lectures as the actual material which will constitute the body of knowledge to be examined. The assumptions of the clientele influence the personnel, who find it increasingly difficult to set questions which give the student opportunity to exercise his judgment or to display the width of his reading in matter not specifically included in his lecture notes. Lecturers even say, 'I can't ask a question on that because I haven't lectured on it this year.' The pattern which develops is a process of feeding information to students in lectures so that they can feed it back in examinations. Even in departments in which tutorial work is done (by no means all in red-brick universities), so dominant is the lecture course-examination nexus that the function of tutorials often appears to be as much custodial as educational—simply to keep students 'at it'. Reliance on the lecture course as the main staple of education has other consequences: it permits students to assume that vacations are free of all obligation to do academic work.

Thus the pattern of instruction becomes a 'feed-in feed-back' system. Notes are 'learned up' for examinations—answers are frequently copy-book recollections of what a lecturer said, or

72

what he is thought to have said. Notes are sometimes passed on by those present to those absent, and some manage to perform quite well in remembering a lecturer's notes, without ever having met the man who has lectured and who marks the papers. This would not matter, of course, if the result were achieved on the strength of wide reading displayed in well-argued answers. But the system as it stands permits smartness to replace both wide knowledge and genuine ability. The occupational skill of students ceases to be intellectuality and becomes the ability to pass examinations without being exposed to a mental discipline. Passing examinations becomes remote from education as students learn the inbuilt disjunction in the system, and how to operate its mechanisms without expenditure of real effort. Being 'smart' and getting a degree whilst avoiding getting an education becomes a more-or-less approved procedure within the student reference-group. In the highly routinized large university this approach becomes the clever way to 'play it'.[12]

Clearly when teaching machines replace teachers, this abbreviation of the educational experience will not only become easier, it will become almost necessary. Our educational pundits will, of course, ignore incidentals of this kind in their bigger concern with statistical evidence of the amount of education which is taking place. As universities grow in size and as the teaching activities are routinized and mechanized, so the examination alone will reveal what the students 'knows'—however notional his knowledge, and regardless of what difference its brief retention makes to him as a person. With continued expansion students who have been 'educated' in this system will be those from whom newer teachers are recruited. Clientele and personnel will now be committed to the smart operation of the mechanized procedures: students will spend their three or four years copying notes, swotting up periodically, sitting examinations, without being very much 'stained' by any educational experience.

THE TUTORIAL SYSTEM

The tutorial system is one feature of English education which commands widespread acceptance in England.[13] Criticisms are usually made only on grounds of expense or 'waste' of teaching resources. In the expansionist case it is a feature which tends to be ignored, or it is assumed that tutorials for five or six might easily replace tutorials for one or two. Given conscientious tutors, the system appears to be the most effective agency for the inculcation of critical discernment, and the transmission of intellectual and cultural concerns. The system is by no means universal in English universities. Thus in Sheffield in 1961 a third of the students were reported to have had neither tutorial nor seminar experience.[14] The technologists, in particular, find no use for tutorials, and again reveal the remoteness of their conception of the needs of the student from that of the university tradition when they say of tutorials, 'In our subjects there is nothing to talk about or to write essays about.' They claim that the associative aspects of the tutorial and the contact of mind with mind are gained in laboratories and drawing offices. But the differences in circumstances is apparent: the association of the tutorial of three or four people (the usual numbers in red-brick universities) with a tutor is a very different experience from the tens of students who work in a laboratory. The whole texture of relationships in the two situations is utterly different.

But even where the tutorial system is in operation it is often under strain. There are doubtless many conscientious tutors, but students I have known well often provide gloomy reports of their tutorials: 'He comes late every week'; 'He seems to be just waiting to get through the hour'; 'He isn't interested in us'. The moral tutor is even less meaningful than the academic tutor. Some see their students once a term when they summon them to an interview. They make no pretence of getting to know their students. The 'Any problems?' approach is common: or the questions: 'How's the grant? How's the digs? How's the girl?' are a matey technique meant to reveal a 'knowing' awareness on the part of the tutor. Instead it is a technique which imposes superficial *bonhomie* on to a situation where it serves only to guarantee that the student will say he has no problems, or none which, in this context, he is prepared to discuss with his tutor. It is an approach which does much to salve the conscience of the tutor without doing much to solve the problems of the student.

The Needs of Students

THE PRESERVATION OF UNIVERSITIES AS EDUCATIONAL AGENCIES

The present condition of our red-brick universities, and their vulnerability in a period of further expansion means that we are faced with a situation of immense wastage of educational resources. Wastage occurs not only when those of high intellectual ability fail to get into university, but when *universities themselves fail* to educate those who do get in. The real issue of the times is not whether we shall have more university education, but whether we shall maintain university education at all. Or shall we maintain the name for something which becomes intrinsically quite different? To expand university education without recognizing the changes which such expansion must entail becomes a piece of political deception of the general public, whose children are promised something which in fact they will not receive.

The consequence of egalitarianism in educational matters is that unequal abilities must appear to be treated equally. Yet education and our whole system of social selection must, to be efficient, rely on discrimination. Democracy and education exist along an uneasy frontier. One can be sure that when education is represented as being democratic, in fact certain concealed manipulative processes necessarily occur in order to maintain the façade of democratic organization. As in the Dodo race everyone must win and everyone must have prizes—so that a subtle manipulative process of redirecting the aspirations of the less able, by counselling, euphemistically-described alternative soft options, and 'gradual disengagement', becomes necessary. The circumstances have been well documented in the case of the American junior college system, where the 'open-door' admission policy entails reliance on 'cooling people out', if any sort of standards are to be maintained.[15] As the apex of an educational system, universities must be discriminatory, must ensure the maintenance of a climate conducive to scholarship, must socialize young people, and eliminate all extraneous threats to their values. Educated men cannot be produced on a crash programme; our most elevated values cannot be entrusted to or transmitted by machines.

From these discussions the following conclusions emerge:

75

Bryan Wilson

(i) To maintain university education at its best we have to be prepared to accept it as a selective, expensive and discriminatory operation. We have to recognize that there is a size beyond which universities become institutionalized at the top and out of control at the bottom. We have to demand heightened dedication from staff and their willingness to give more time to students. Lecturers must face the fact that their role is not a job but is a commitment to a way of life in which human values are centrally entrenched. It may be argued that to demand that more time be given to students (not necessarily to be spent in, or only in, teaching) would be to jeopardize the research work of academic staff. So it might, within the context of the university itself. But then we must have the imagination to establish separate research institutes—centres like Ottawa for the sciences and like Palo Alto for the arts and social sciences. We must be prepared to arrange generous secondments of staff for two, three or five years, according to need, and to ensure graduated promotions between these institutions and universities proper. In return for facilities of this kind, we must demand a much higher commitment to students from these privileged classes during the normal course of their university careers.

(ii) We must also be prepared to place in separate institutions those disciplines which make demands which can be ill accorded in universities. The technologies have different requirements, sometimes even appear to espouse quite alien theories of education itself. Ought they not to have institutions where they can develop with minimal tension, and with facilities specifically designed for their needs? They may argue that such institutions would lack the prestige of universities. One has yet to be convinced that in contemporary society academic learning commands such high social prestige—the pay and social standing of academics suggests otherwise. The lack of imagination in the Robbins Report is that it failed to envisage the multiplicity and diversity of possible educational provision. It seemed stuck with the university model and assumed its universal applicability to all forms of social training. One would have liked to see proposals for many types of institutions of higher education, all organized for the needs of particular types of discipline. The opposition to the expansion of universities need not be, and in this case is not, the opposition to the expansion of higher education as such. The final argument of the technologists (and of others) is that the technologists gain something of the general culture from being in association with the arts and the natural sciences. One assumes that the argument applies mainly to students—that technologist lecturers do not at this stage feel still the need to pick up gleanings of culture from their arts colleagues. Yet the assumption that the dust of culture falls from arts students to technologists is highly questionable. To put the historian and the civil engineer into one room in a hall of residence is to see that they talk of things other than the academic: often reciprocal disdain is increased by such contact, unless there is someone in the situation who is prepared to discover a common language and a set of common interests. That can be done only in the context of a community—a relatively small hall in which individuals can be well known, and their particular interests, needs and experience be taken into account.

(iii) The tutorial system seems indispensable to the maintenance of the values of English universities, but it is something which must exist at more than the paper level. One is impressed, as a newcomer to Oxford, by the thoroughness which is induced when reports have to be made in detail about students by tutors to the colleges to which those students belong. The divergence of allegiance, the separation of the examining and the tutoring agencies (and sometimes of the college responsible for the student and the man who actually teaches him) appears to provide a machinery which ensures that a tutor gets to know his pupil. This is something which does not always happen when the relationship takes place within a department, where the difficulty of colleague-relationships prevents effective checking and criticism of each other's work, which would of course be contrary to the spirit of the university system. In Oxford the cross-checks appear to operate more naturally: there is, too, a multiplicity of tutors which has advantages for the pupil, and provides the tutor with some incentive to do his work more conscientiously.

(iv) Halls of residence can be a context in which the cultural and intellectual concerns of the university can be sustained. The halls of residence have recently been under attack. On the one hand they are expensive, and on the other they imply a moral responsibility for students which not all in universities are willing to undertake. Blocks of bed-sitters are recommended as being both cheaper and 'more popular with students'. Popularity with students chances to coincide with expediency, and so the university prepares to surrender the educational commitment of its concern with residence for something which is justified as 'more in the spirit of the times'—whatever that may mean. In fact it means the abandonment of concern for students, and the replacement of cumbersome and difficult regard for their welfare as individuals by something which is administratively more convenient. Administration begins to replace educational concern, and this, of course, is the trend once organizations accept a policy of expansion into mass institutions. The new blocks of bed-sitters and the very big halls of residence (the skyscrapers) are themselves a surrender to the institutionalization of even living conditions. The hall, as a place in which people broaden their educational experience and learn to make education part of life, is one of the facilities of universities which has been suddenly almost abandoned in the past few years: quickly it has become 'old fashioned'. It projects no image, being committed to abiding values rather than to modern gimmicks. This is not to suggest that all halls have ideally fulfilled their possible functions. Some have been too hierarchic, maintaining status-divisions, initiations and the dominance of cliques—either with or without the approval of wardens.[16] Some have an imposed unnatural and forced formality on public occasions, without realizing that high formality of the authoritarian kind invariably leads to high informality of the rebellious kind. There has sometimes been a failure to realize that an even level of appropriate formality has more dignity and more value for students—in revealing to them civilized habits which can be maintained in daily life—than has the occasional high formality of the parade.

But the hall *can* be a community of a unique kind, in which university values can inform a way of life, in which individuals can express individuality, acquire personal dignity and experience security in an assured context. Tensions will inevitably exist, both inter-personally and institutionally, but halls can be places in which individuals learn to contain tensions and to deal with them. Young people can be treated as adults and induced to make adult responses; they can be induced to live up to their own best pretences and aspirations about themselves, so that these become natural to them. The concerns of the community can become the shared concerns of warden and students, from decisions about domestic details to wider ranging community concerns. This is to encourage student participation—but not to sell out to the demands of the youth culture. Individual liberty can be provided in a context of sustained concern and shared involvement. People must be free enough to learn by making fools of themselves, but in the secure context of a community this freedom is valuable rather than deleterious. There must be a high degree of formal and informal communication which occurs within a clear structure of relationships, in which wardens never cease to be wardens, never try to become 'one of the boys' or to gain confidence by undue familiarity. They must get beyond inviting people in for sherry once a term on a rota system, but they must also know how to draw the line at accepting invitations to go to the pub with particular groups. They cannot afford to become identified with particular cliques; nor must they be remote, status-conscious individuals; they must wear authority lightly if, ultimately, firmly. Their business is to support students in coping—academically, administratively (and this becomes an increasing problem for students who find it difficult even to understand the administrative operation of the university) and socially.

A hall should be a place where learning can proceed and liberalize the specialisms of the university; it should promote activities which are consonant with the university's purposes— hikes, concerts, talks, poetry reading, music, exhibitions, as well as the dances, social occasions and sport which students will largely organize for themselves. It must provide a context of shared enterprises in which the various talents and skills of its members can be drawn into use. All of this makes it easier for engineers to talk to historians, the more so if equally new cultural experiences are being presented to them from time to time: conversation in 'living groups' gravitates quickly to banalities unless someone (a warden or his deputy) constantly works at it, introducing new ideas and opening up new vistas. In this context there need be no establishment of what we shall no doubt soon hear canvassed as an inevitable consequence of mass institutions—a counselling service. In a good hall the warden learns about a student's problems almost before the individual student himself. Counselling is simply a part of the free flow of discussion between warden and individual hall member, without there being much need for formal interviews. Knowing the problem means knowing the man, and only sustained interaction can provide that knowledge. This is the basis on which counselling can take place, and on which proper testimonials can be written (one wonders how the teaching machines will manage that, but perhaps these, too, will be routinized into a series of three or four standard forms of letters of recommendation!). All of these facilities are, of course, part of the *small* hall —only there can meaningful inter-personal relationships operate throughout the community; only in small pools can each individual have the experience of being the big fish. The hall must be a distinctive institution, and its operation cannot be conducted on the model of a hotel, a hostel, a hospital, a hostelry, a sport pavilion or a holiday-home. The small hall can be more than a mere ancillary service to the university, it can and does become a most valued and meaningful part of university education: 'You know, Warden, if I hadn't been in Hall my time at this university would have been pretty miserable.'

The small hall might be the relief from the big university, if we *must* have big universities.[17] It could be the place where individuals are not reduced to punch-cards, are not manipulated by increasingly mechanized devices. The demands of administration become necessarily dominant in large institutions, but education is a subtle, complex and highly individuated experience which surrenders reluctantly to administrative imperatives. As administrative pressures grow, so the human considerations in education, to which I attach primary importance, will be gradually reduced and perhaps eliminated. One wonders whether this is a legitimate development in an educational context, whether it is not ultimately the betrayal of the values of education. Might one not hope that in a mass society universities should remain small enough to permit personal relationships to exist and the shared experience of intellectual and cultural concerns to become the radical alternative to administrative expediency?

The Needs of Students

1. See the evidence presented in the University Grants Committee report 'The Use of Vacations by Students' (H.M.S.O., London, 1963).

2. The incidence of hooliganism is not, of course, recorded by those who undertake research on universities (who are themselves usually employed by universities and therefore sometimes somewhat involved in seeking to project an image not unfavourable to expansion). Newspapers (especially student newspapers) often reveal the surprising extent of student hooliganism. I quote only two examples. In the autumn of 1963 the students of Leeds University Union contemplated banning all students of the Manchester College of Science and Technology from the Leeds University Union after sports teams visiting Leeds from Manchester were alleged to have indulged in 'an orgy of hooliganism' in which glasses, bottles and microphones were broken and cigarette machines damaged. The police were called in when 'students started to tilt concrete mixers'. So strongly did the Leeds students feel about the matter that they took the unusual step of a letter of protest to the Principal of the Manchester College. My quotation is from *The Yorkshire Post* report which was written by a former President of the Leeds University Union. In Sheffield, on 14th May 1963, the following incident is recorded, not without a note of pride, in *Darts*, the newspaper of the Sheffield University Students Union: 'Thursday night proved an eventful night for three of the Halls. . . . Inebriated members of Stephenson Hall visited Halifax (Hall) and Crewe (Hall) . . . (where) windows were bombarded by plants uprooted from the garden. The reason for the celebration was the Foundation Dinner at Stephenson, where gallons of free beer were flowing in such quantities that the residents were able to prime themselves for an evening's heavy drinking in one of Sheffield's many public-houses. When all the food and drink was gone, Stephenson, dressed to kill in dinner jackets and gowns, rode into town *en masse*. . . . As they strode along, they left clear signs that they had passed by. The times of all the "No Waiting" signs had been altered, the University Car Park sign had disappeared, and several women, met *en route*, were molested. . . . Hearing a din outside Crewe, the Warden of Stephenson hastened to the scene, only to find his charges deflowering the grounds and hurling plants at the windows. . . . His answer to their behaviour was to ban all free beer on subsequent occasions.'

3. The limitations of this kind of research and the biases, conscious and unconscious, which it permits, might be illustrated by three examples. (i) Robert Peers, *Fact and Possibility in English Education* (London, 1963), appears not to be aware of the extent to which a question 'framed somewhat differently' throws into doubt the significance of his results. I quote: '. . . an overwhelming proportion of those who expressed an opinion welcomed liberal studies as part of their professional education—at one of the institutions 84·4 per cent. . . . The question was framed somewhat differently at the second institution and here 51·5 per cent regarded liberal studies as helpful for their specialist professional education' (p. 111). It becomes evident that results sometimes hang on an almost incidental choice of works. (ii) Mr. Peter Marris investigated student preferences for different types of

81

accommodation among final-year students at Leeds and Southampton (final year is, of course, the year when preference for hall is likely to be lowest, since more students have either left halls, come to terms with the fact that they cannot be admitted to halls, or are beginning to seek a more independent arrangement as they get older). He shows that 27 per cent and 33 per cent of final-year students at these universities preferred accommodation in halls. Mr. Marris ignored in his presentation (*New Society*, 33 [14th May 1963], pp. 8–10) a 1961 survey for Sheffield University in which 44 per cent of students in all years (finalists showing no special difference from those of other years) stated a preference for hall from a choice of eight types of accommodation (P. H. Mann and G. Mills, 'Living and Learning at Redbrick', *Universities Quarterly*, 16, 1 (Dec., 1961), pp. 19–35). He preferred instead a 1957 survey of Birmingham, the results of which were rather more in accordance with the case he was making. Mr. Marris, like many of the investigators into university accommodation, does not himself favour halls. (iii) The Report of the Committee on Student Accommodation at the University of Leeds preferred the response to questionnaires about the type of accommodation for which students had applied to the actual documentary evidence of the filed application forms. They preferred retrospective rationalizations to actual evidence of behaviour. The committee noted the discrepancy in the case of the women's hall particularly, where 'all the women in hall (in their sample) . . . when asked whether if they were starting university life again from the beginning they would choose to live in lodgings or in hall, said they would prefer to be in hall' (p. 81). From girls in lodgings they had an almost equal unanimity in favour of lodgings. From the tone of the report the committee was loath to come to the conclusion, on the strength of this evidence, that the selection procedures employed by wardens were so startlingly satisfactory. But curiously they failed to draw the other conclusion, that actual data of behaviour from documentary sources (the application forms) is more reliable than questionnaire responses on which they were so heavily reliant. From these illustrations it becomes apparent that market research techniques must be regarded with some suspicion even on technical grounds.

4. The foregoing paragraph and, in somewhat amended form, several other paragraphs first appeared in my article 'Youth Culture and the University', *The Cambridge Review*, vol. 85, No. 2059 (26th October 1963), pp. 50–2, which I reproduce here by kind permission of the editors.

5. Thefts from students of valuables, clothing and even lecture notes are a commonplace in universities. Sometimes these matters reach such proportions that, despite the reluctance of university officials to risk publicity which might tarnish the university's image, matters are placed in the hands of the police. Thefts occur not only from students, but also by students from the university. *Redbrick*, published by the students of Birmingham University (a journal interestingly reminiscent in style of the *Daily Mirror*, which, rather than *The Times* or *The Guardian*, appears to be the model for student journalism) reported on 20th November 1963, that 'pilfering from Catering Department has soared to an all-time high. . . . Since the beginning of this term 40 per cent of the knives—£62 worth—over 25 per cent of the forks, and more than half the spoons, worth £17, have been stolen from the Union's

seven service points. The figures for cups and other implements are similar. . . . The refectory also has its troubles. Over £800 worth of cutlery and cups have been borrowed . . . since the refectory opened last year.' The same issue of this journal reports: 'Third-year students S . . . L . . . reports having a wallet containing £15 stolen from his case in the Library cloakrooms.' There is also a story that money from the student newspaper collecting box in the Medical School has twice been stolen. Loyalty to the University and even to the Union appears to be lacking.

6. The phenomenon is not, of course, confined to redbrick universities. An unidentified 'Oxbridge undergraduate' began his substantial article in the *Sunday Times*, 13th October 1963, 'While there has been much talk recently about the structure and organisation of universities, little account seems to have been taken of the life and problems of students themselves. . . . They are either regarded as having the happiest time of their lives, or just raw material for whatever production line the experts feel is best for the country. Yet, anyone who has come into close contact with undergraduates must be struck by the sizeable proportion who seem ill-adjusted, bored and frustrated. For many of the most intelligent and imaginative students, university has apparently not provided the intellectual stimulus and all-round education that it claims.'

7. It is somewhat difficult to understand the attraction of siting universities in industrial areas, except for the political appeal of showing that they do not belong exclusively to the snob environment of cathedral cities. Mr. Harold Wilson said at the Labour Party Conference (*The Times*, 2nd October 1963): '. . . let us try and see that more (universities) are sited in industrial areas where they can, in some way, reflect the pulsating throb of local industry and work in partnership with the new industries we seek to create.' But apart from the less congenial atmosphere for study, the problem of digs, parking, traffic, noise, dirt, inavailability of local labour, absence of cultural facilities, there is also the important fact that most academics do not like to live in industrial environments, and that in a period when their specialized labour is certain to be scarce, universities in industrial cities are unlikely to attract the best staff. Mr. Wilson's point was perhaps not really made for the sake of universities, but for the sake of industrial areas, since, according to *The Times*, he went on to say that 'not enough thought has been given to the establishment of the new universities which could help to revitalize areas.' This statement reveals little concern for education. It reminds one of the claims of Stevenage when, some years ago, it sought to attract a university and advanced as grounds the significance of a university for local trade and the opportunity it would provide for local architects who needed to have something big 'to have a go at'.

8. The importance of this principle has been appreciated at York where the authorities have rejected the idea of one central Union in favour of a plurality of smaller student associations based on residential colleges. There can be little doubt of the superiority of this arrangement in the modern large university in terms of its value for the individual. The Unions elsewhere are, of course, likely to persist, despite their declining value to individual students as universities grow larger. They continue simply by force of institutional persistence and the automatic receipt of income collected for them

by the authorities as an obligatory part of student fees. Much of the money is spent on relatively few student athletes. The Unions are, of course, supported by the equally small numbers of politically-conscious students who use the mass-organization as an arena in which to test their political strength and discover power. Even within its first term of operation the decision against a central Union at York was the subject of bitter comment by the Presidents of other university Unions.

9. Some of the newer universities have been well aware of this problem. The University of Keele has, since its inception, insisted on studies spanning three faculties, and the University of Sussex has deliberately abolished departments in the attempt to 'redraw the map of learning'.

10. Thus Professor P. M. S. Blackett asserts that 'the advantages of a large university over a small one are becoming increasingly recognized. In many ways they are certainly more efficient and provide a better education because of the breadth of knowledge found in a large staff' (*The Times*, 9th October 1963). We are not informed what is meant by efficiency in this context, nor how it is related to the individual's educational experience. Or is the 'increasing recognition' merely a euphemism for saying 'it is becoming increasingly expedient to believe'? Professor Blackett continues: 'In my youth the absolute pre-eminence of Oxford and Cambridge lay not nearly so much as some think in the college system and spiritual effects of medieval architecture and green lawns, but . . . (in the fact that) they were so big; this meant they had a lot of distinguished staff.' But how big were Oxford and Cambridge when Professor Blackett was a youth? In 1923–4 Oxford had 4,163 students. It was thus little more than half as big as present-day Manchester or Leeds—even before the expansion which Robbins demands! He continues: 'In general any university which wants to be distinguished in learning and research will have to plan for a large number of undergraduates, for only so will they get from the Government the money to buy distinguished staff.' This emphasis on the mercenary quality of academic incentive reveals the fact that it is not *bigness* which attracts staff, but the persistence of the absurd relationship between size and income, which is today a hang-over from an ancient system of income distribution in our universities.

11. The argument for larger universities which I seek here to refute, point by point, has various advocates whose assertions are essentially similar. I take them here in the order in which they were put forward by Godfrey Hodgson in 'Wisconsin Shows the Way—a commentary on the Robbins Report' in *The Observer*, 27th October 1963.

12. The system comes to resemble that observed by Malcolm Bradbury (to whom I am indebted for this point) at the large University of Indiana, where fraternities and sororities keep highly-rated essays on file, so that when the theme is set again, students need neither read nor think but simply copy up the essay which made the grade before. For a more general set of impressions see Mr. Bradbury's article in *The Twentieth Century*, vol. 161, no. 950 (February 1957), pp. 116–24).

13. Students appear to value the tutorial system very highly. This has always been my own experience of student opinion, although they have often found individual tutors deficient. A survey of Manchester University

students, directed by Salvino Busuttil (Manchester, 1962), reports: 'Some 65·2 per cent of the sample were in favour of having more tutorials, and we have reason to believe that a good many of the 22·9 per cent who gave no answer shared the same opinion. . . . Tutorials, we were told time and again by students, were considered to be the most valuable part of university training' (p. 29).

14. The 'Memorandum to the University Grants Committee' of the Students' Union, University of Sheffield (March 1961), expresses, though curiously written, the strong appreciation by students of the tutorial system: 'An overwhelming majority of students express the desire for both an increase in instruction in the form of seminars and individual tutorials. In our opinion the seminar and tutorial systems are essentially complementary to the lecture system: the latter being solely a one-way process. Only in either a seminar or tutorial are members of the teaching staff able to judge the individual needs of their students and therefore teach accordingly. We therefore recommend most strongly that such methods of instruction should be implemented at the earliest possible time, as apart from its obvious merit on academic grounds, these systems make an invaluable contribution to staff-student understanding.'

15. See Burton R. Clark, 'The Cooling Out Function in Higher Education', *American Journal of Sociology*, LXV (May 1960), pp. 569–76; also reprinted in A. H. Halsey, Jean Floud and C. A. Anderson, *Education, Economy and Society* (Glencoe, Ill., 1961).

16. For an account of a system which one has seen with variations elsewhere, see the revealing article by Anthony Giddens, 'Aspects of the Social Structure of a University Hall of Residence', *Sociological Review*, 8 (July 1960), pp. 97–108.

17. The attitude of students towards large universities, and their appreciation of small units with which they can more readily identify themselves, can be seen in Ferdinand Zweig, *The Student in an Age of Anxiety: A Survey of Oxford and Manchester Students* (London: Heinemann, 1963), pp. 98–101. 'At least half of the sample [of the students at Manchester] had only praise for the university . . . 53 out of 103 students "enjoyed", "enjoyed thoroughly" or "enjoyed very much" their university life. . . . *Those who had only praise for university life were often in residence in Halls* . . . or were students in small departments with a more integrated social life. . . . There were 34 other students who were critical of the university. . . . "It's too big and impersonal"; "Too large and overcrowded"; "Too cramped and restricted"; "Drab and dirty with nothing to take you out of yourself"; "Too formal, there is little personal interest on the part of the staff"; "Too much concentration on getting a degree instead of getting culture and education"; "The teaching's impersonal, a gulf exists between staff and students. In my department you can go right through the course without ever speaking to the professor". . . . There were 16 other students who voiced their criticism very strongly, disapproving of this type of university altogether. . . . "A depressing place. No bond, no pride, no sense of belonging." This criticism often came from students in big departments where the personal contact with the staff is often lost and which give an impression of overcrowding.' (My italics.)

Dr. Wilson fears above all the dilution of the abiding human values which it is the university's task to transmit. He sees 'the technologists' as an agency of dilution and therefore would separate them from the universities with whose purpose they are in ill accord. There are two kinds of riposte to this. Even if they could be kept unspotted, what would it profit the universities to cut themselves off from an impulse which is a vital and characteristic part of this age's genius? Would not the humane values atrophy and die? For, in the second place, the question must be asked: Is it not of urgent importance that the very civilizing values Dr. Wilson is defending should be transmitted to the technologists as well? To many it appears that the very values themselves cannot be saved unless, embodied in new forms, they permeate new types of higher education. Later in this book Mr. Maitland-Edwards claims that colleges of technology are already truly educating institutions who, at this very time, are driving forward with immense verve in their task of fusing old and new values. Perhaps the ivory tower is an engaging myth of the past, for we are being forced into a position where 'the academic community and the rest of society will be more directly involved with and affected by each other than ever before'. Unless the academic community is in constant and fruitful intercourse with the technological society it must help to civilize and lead, Nemesis will descend on both. So argues Dr. Jenkins.

M. R.

4

The Educated Society

DANIEL JENKINS

The term 'the educated society' is used in this paper to refer not merely to the academic community, those directly engaged in the work of formal education as their main activity, but to the kind of general organization of common life into which all industrially and educationally advanced countries appear to be moving. It is the kind of society in which paper qualifications obtained through formal education increasingly become the chief factors in determining the function and status of most people. To echo the term created by Peter Drucker, who has been one of the first to call attention to the significance of these developments in the life of the U.S.A., we are rapidly approaching the age, not of 'economic' or 'industrial' man but of 'educated' or, at least, 'educationally qualified' man.

This process of expansion is still only at its early stages. Education has already become the largest single employer of labour in the U.S.A. and most other industrially advanced countries are likely to reach a similar position within the next generation. Like many others, I believe that the report of the Robbins Committee errs on the side of caution rather than otherwise in estimating the amount of expansion of institutions of higher education which will be possible and which society will demand in the years before us. Those who view this situation with alarm, whether for good reasons or bad, and who make efforts to resist or slow down the process of expansion, especially in relation to universities, fail to show much sense of the way in which large-scale social movements develop and gather momentum. This failure may be due to the combination of naivety, indifference and class-consciousness with which many British academic persons have traditionally regarded the wider social context of their work, and to their studied ignorance of sociology.

For it is manifest that the movement towards this enormous educational expansion has not taken place simply as the result of a capricious change of social mood. This is not to deny that there is an element of the merely fashionable in it. All large-scale movements are open to this danger—the popularity of church-going in many parts of the U.S.A. provides a very good analogy—and there are few things over which people are more disposed to try to keep up with the established trend and the current popular social expectation than over the education of their children. But such an immense enterprise could not possibly maintain itself, at the vast and growing expense which it involves, and do so in many countries with differing social histories, unless there were deeper reasons for it than that.

The most obvious and important reason is that it is necessitated by our great scientific and technical expansion. It is clearly incontestable that this is the essential condition of the existence of 'the educated society', without which it could never have begun to emerge. Whatever else we may need, we certainly need more scientists, technicians and technologists. Yet it is essential from the outset to see that, just because we need these, we also need people with many other skills and abilities besides. The roots of scientific and technological expansion lie deeper in the soil of humanity than some of their practitioners imagine. It has yet to be proved that science and technology can expand indefinitely, and do so in creative ways, unless those who practise them, and the general society of which they are part, have a broad and humane outlook. Creativity in science is more intimately related to creativity in the arts, humanities and religion, than those concerned only with enjoying the short-term fruits of scientific discovery can readily see. As is now widely recognized, if society is divided into two cultures, both are likely to suffer. More than this, the greater and more easily-produced wealth which is created by industry based on science and technology and the kind of society inevitably produced by it, create the need for specialized services which can be most easily met by formal education. This is partly because this wealth produces more leisure and the need to fill up this leisure in the most worth-while ways possible. Milton Mayer, in his book *Our Schools*, has pointed out that one important factor in keeping ever-growing numbers of young people in school and college in the U.S.A. has been that they have not been wanted on the labour market, except in casual and insignificant roles, and that, to put it at its lowest, they are better off in educational institutions than anywhere else. With growing efficiency and automation, the same is likely to apply ever more widely. But it is much more that this kind of highly industrialized society demands a very high standard of education on many levels.

This is a point whose importance can hardly be exaggerated, because it is often not adequately grasped both by those within the academic community and by those outside. Highly industrialized society, which operates with an elaborate technology, is a quite new type of society, without a parallel in human history. It is very highly organized. It demands a great deal of detailed specialization, yet the specialists must be in close contact with each other and their work must be co-ordinated. Its parts are interdependent and control over them has to be centralized. It is also expansionist and large-scale in its very nature. It is also mobile to an extent never known before, especially among those holding positions carrying any responsibility. Science, technology and industrialization are the great revolutionary forces of the modern world, far more so than any political movements. They uproot people from old-established communities and settled ways, with all the indirect educational influences which these have provided. It is much more difficult in this kind of situation for the individual to accept the guidance of those in traditional positions of authority and he has to make a much more conscious and deliberate effort to participate in the life of the community. That participation, in its turn, often has to take new and strange forms and to involve a host of relationships with people whose background and ways of thinking may be unfamiliar to him.

All this means that people have to learn a whole host of skills and to acquire attitudes which are quite new and foreign to all but a small minority. Communication is vital in this kind of society. Men have to learn how to speak and to achieve understanding, often through highly complicated new media, with others whom they may never see face to face. They have, for severely practical reasons, to know more about others' languages and cultures than ever before. They need infinitely greater library and information services than simpler societies were able to manage with. New professions develop as a result of the complexity of modern life—those of town planners and transport experts and market researchers and the like. New and higher standards of design in relation to an ever-growing number of objects are required—decisive proof, if any were required, that it is impossible to draw any hard and fast line between the spheres of the scientist and the artist. Along with these goes the need for greater social skills—skill in political relationships, skill in establishing mutual confidence with people at a distance or with very different backgrounds from one's own, skill in creating worth-while relationships in communities most of whose members are extremely mobile. No society in history has needed people of greater maturity of mind and flexibility of outlook than ours. In so far as these are produced by training in the arts and humanities, they provide the strongest of practical justifications for those who argue that these sides of the academic community must expand along with the scientific and technological if we are not to destroy ourselves.

Those who insist that the great expansion of educational institutions under this kind of pressure exposes them to great dangers are, of course, right. It is essential that the nature of these should be fully stated and that efforts should be made to overcome them. Yet all who are conscious of these dangers must realize this. They are inherent in the nature of the kind of society we have. There is no prospect of our having, in our time or in any foreseeable future, a different kind of society. It is formal education itself which is the chief instrument in the hands of the community for minimizing and overcoming these dangers. Unless those who are responsible for formal education, and this is especially true of those engaged in higher education, see their social role in a much more positive and active way than many of them seem so far disposed to do, there is no obvious way in which the evils of our kind of society can be prevented from overwhelming those elements in it which are excellent. The fate which already threatens our world will overtake it. We shall die of a combination of boredom and inaction, engendered by a surfeit of goods and services provided for the convenience of productive organizations and wished upon us by advertisement, with all our criticism anticipated by public relations experts and all our efforts to dig deeper into life shown to be pointless in the universal self-satisfaction. We shall die in this

Daniel Jenkins

way, that is, only if we succeed in avoiding a more violent fate.

In earlier times, those in the world of education could reasonably rely on those in other fields to occupy themselves with activities on which the general well-being of society depended, without themselves being too much concerned with them. Henceforward, however, this will less and less be true. Unless, for example, the universities and related institutions produce people who are artistically and scientifically creative, it is hard to see, given the efficiency of our processes of educational selection, where else they can come from.

All this means an entirely different approach to the relation between the academic community and the rest of society from that which has been normative in the past. Right through the nineteenth century, as Drucker has pointed out, higher education—in contrast to what was firmly described as elementary education—was thought of primarily as education for leisure, and therefore as relevant only to a small minority of the population. Liberal education was part of the equipment of a gentleman. It enabled him to be a cultivated, all-round person, who did not need to obtain training for his livelihood from his education, since the assumption was that his livelihood was assured in other ways. It is true that with the characteristic English genius for the modification of ideals to face new situations, this liberal education was increasingly conceived of in such a way as to enable people to be in a position to earn their living should the need arise, as it more and more and quite inevitably did. It is this which lies behind the engaging Oxford myth, which still appears to perpetuate itself with surprising vigour in such traditional citadels of amateurism as the Cabinet and the Treasury, that the man who has read Greats, without having done anything so vulgar as to have undergone any training, can turn his mind to anything. Nowadays, however, for most people, it is impossible to maintain this amiable semi-pretence any more. The education one has received affects one's job and one's status in society more directly than ever before, and increasingly more directly than any other single consideration.

It also means that we must accept the fact that the academic community and the rest of society will be more directly involved with and affected by each other than ever before. Education, like war, has now become too important to be left to the experts. What happens in schools and colleges affects what happens in the great world outside too directly for those in politics and economic life, let alone anxious parents, to be indifferent to them. Likewise, schools and colleges have to take a lively and active interest in what is happening in the world around them and to try, in the ways appropriate to them, to influence that world, if what they do in their own internal life is to have any significance.

This, in its turn, means that the question of academic freedom and independence has to be looked at in a fresh context. It was never more important than it is today that schools, colleges and universities should have genuine freedom, but it cannot be thought of in realistic terms unless the implications of the rest of society's lively interest in them are frankly faced. The general community pays enormous sums for education and academic institutions cannot expect to maintain their freedom unless they go to a great deal of trouble to justify themselves and to explain why their freedom and independence are important. Similarly, in fast-moving and restless modern society, a measure of detachment and reasonable peace to get on with its own work will be absolutely essential to the effectiveness of the academic community, but these can only be obtained if the members of that community realize how much they are involved with the rest of society. They will be unable to think of themselves as inhabiting a place of retreat from the ordinary world but will know that they belong to a characteristic and important part of that world, with a powerful direct influence upon the rest.

With the advent of 'the educated society' much more attention than ever before will also have to be given to the question of the relationship between the highly educated and the other groups in society on wider levels than of those between institutions. These aspects of the relationship seem to me to call particularly for more inquiry.

First, it seems inevitable that the highly educated will have to have a much more acute awareness of their social obligations and a much more precise notion of how to fulfil them. This refers not only to those who actually work in academic institutions but also to their graduates at work in the wider world. They owe their privileged position very directly to the readiness of the rest of society to support them in academic pursuits. Their style of life will increasingly determine that of large parts of the rest of the community in the future. The force of this has been partly obscured since the war because of the sudden prosperity of the relatively uneducated, more particularly those unmarried young people who start work early, but nothing is more certain, given peace, than that this will become less and less true. What kind of an example in social responsibility are our educated young people receiving from their seniors and what kind of *relevant* example are they offering to their less well-educated contemporaries? We hear much of the limitations of popular culture in these days. We do not hear so much of the fact that one of the troubles with it is that the highly educated are often content to be assimilated into it without discrimination and sometimes only too ready to purvey and exploit it to their own advantage. It is doubtful whether, with the advent of 'the educated society', centres of higher education can show the slightest degree of complacency about the social attitudes and styles of life of large numbers of their products.

Similarly, the professional ideals and the conduct of the professional organizations of the highly qualified need a degree of critical scrutiny they have so far never received. As 'the educated society' develops, the power of these organizations is certain to grow, to a far greater extent than that of the industrial unions, whose power, indeed, will probably diminish. The irresponsible conduct of the American Medical Association over the Medicare proposals is an alarming indication, of which the whole educated world should take careful note, of how self-interest can lead a group of educated men to deny all that education and their professional ideal should have taught them. Fortunately, English life cannot as yet show such a disgraceful episode but it would have been refreshing, for example, if the representatives of universities had been able to say to the N.I.C. that, whatever salary modifications may be necessary from time to time, they lead such full and happy lives that they do not need salaries as large as those of members of the administrative grade of the Civil Service.

It is vital that the highly educated should show restraint in the use of their increasingly great powers in relation to the rest of society. It is true that the dangers of 'meritocracy' arise in modern Britain, as in modern America, only to a strictly limited extent. In both countries, the 'mediocracy' is built in to too many positions of privilege for it to be readily overthrown. But the gulf between those who are highly qualified and those who are not is bound to grow in modern society unless conscious and determined efforts are made to bridge it. It is no use pretending that those who are not selected to receive the kind of education which leads to attractive jobs and status will regard themselves as anything else than failures. It is the humbug of the successful, which deceives only themselves, to refuse to admit this. If the educated use their growing social power only to gain more privileges for themselves and to underline their superiority at every turn, disparaging the capacities of their less educated neighbours while they also exploit their weakness and failure, we are saving up serious trouble for ourselves in the future.

Secondly, the question must be asked with new urgency of how far educational institutions, and again particularly those of higher education, are adequately equipped to be the training-grounds for life in 'the educated society'. Oxford and Cambridge have, for several generations, had a unique formative influence upon the Civil Service, the political life and some of the professions in this country, although nothing like as large an influence upon its industrial and financial life. Henceforward, nearly everyone who is likely to have a position of influence in society is going to spend his life until he is twenty-one or older in an educational institution. His attitude towards life will be formed by the institution as never before, especially when we bear in mind what was said earlier about mobility and the break-up of classes and closely-knit neighbourhoods. As far as most universities are concerned, they are organized chiefly in order to train people for scholarly research. Is this sufficient in view of the social duties which are being inescapably laid upon their members?

This is not to say that the virtues of the academic community as it has developed in our own time—its emphasis on verifiable knowledge, as scholarly humility and patience, on the importance of criticism and of economy in the use of materials and on the constant raising of standards—are not essential to the well-being of our kind of society. They certainly are, and the fact that they are is a powerful reminder that society needs not only technical skills but all the qualities and resources of the academic mind at its best if it is to survive in the kind of world which its technical skills create. These virtues, however, will not find adequate expression and may indeed become corrupted unless the academic community recognizes its limitations and dangers—the arrogance, the indecisiveness, the pedantry and the lack of proportion—which quickly become manifest when it is isolated and inbred.

These limitations and dangers can only be overcome if there is a new freedom and flexibility in the relations between the different parts of the academic enterprise and between them all and the rest of the society. If schools and colleges erect unnecessary barriers between each other and limit the social sympathy of their products, they are failing badly. Snobbery is a sign of fundamental educational incompetence. Where do some of Britain's 'top' institutions stand in the light of this fact? We also urgently need a fresh and more positive understanding of the vocational element in education. A very large part of education is vocational, but people are often reluctant to admit it and do not approach it constructively enough. It may be one of the great insights brought by the Biblical understanding of man that there need be no ultimate contradiction between liberal and vocational education. Provided the job fulfils a worth-while human need and is seen in enough depth and in a wide enough context, preparation for it helps to give a sense of purpose and the discipline of life as it is to academic study, and to guard against the dangers of indecision and triviality.

Above all, however, those who lead the academic community need a strong awareness of human solidarity and the interdependence of the worth-while parts of life. R. H. Tawney's familiar words apply here more directly than anywhere else that the clever men are impressed with their differences from their fellows and wise men are conscious of their resemblances to them. It is more important to bear this in mind because it is probably true to say that, in our present confused situation, society is often best served by making educational institutions as unlike much of the rest of the community as possible. They can only do this safely if they take part in the general life of the community. This means that they should recognize their responsibility for what is purveyed through the large-scale public media of communication such as broadcasting and the press, and that they should see the importance for themselves of the style of life of the non-academic members of the community. In the 'educated society' academic and non-academic people alike are members one of another as never before. It is not merely that they have complementary gifts; it is also that they must learn how to share these gifts. This must mean that the academic man must have the sympathy and humility which will enable him to take trouble to help the majority of people to be critical and discriminating and responsible, and to enjoy life in a world which is even more bewildering to them than it is to the academic man. If he fails to do this, he will be making his contribution to turning the majority of his fellows into 'the mass'. This will not merely be the betrayal of his own responsibility, it will also be the beginning of the end of the academic community and 'the educated society' themselves.

The health of the academic community has depended heavily in the past upon the general health of the society of which it is part. This will be even more true in the future, with the important qualification that henceforward the academic community itself will have a much larger role in determining the character of the general life of society. Self-questioning is an essential element in intellectual inquiry and there are many important questions to which conclusive answers cannot be given, but it is hard to deny that there is an element of false detachment from an inescapable human situation in the scepticism concerning ultimate convictions sometimes displayed by members of the academic community. It is easy to hold attitudes about these matters in academic isolation without having to face their full social implications. With the advent of the 'educated society' we shall have to ask very carefully where the springs of genuine intellectual vitality are to be found. It is not clear that they are to be found within the 'educational process' itself. In our society, they have generally been found close to Christian or other religious conviction, and it is not yet obvious that they can be kept running indefinitely if men move very far away from those convictions. The relation between faith and learning is neither simple nor direct but it appears all the same to be an intimate one. It has been observed that the story of many families has been that the first generation has been godly, the second learned, the third wealthy, and the fourth has had no adjective attached to it because it has vanished from significant history. Could this be the fate of the 'educated society' itself because those who are its chief beneficiaries have been content to say in their pride, 'By my own might and the strength of mine own arm have I gotten this wealth'?

Part Two

THE STUDENT EXPERIENCE

The academic teaching purpose is essentially a human one: to transmit the human past to the human present in order to make the human future. It is concerned with the transmission of learning, not its advancement. It represents a vital human activity—that of communication. In a living process of communication it is the whole person that is communicated—not just the teacher's organized stock of knowledge, but his enthusiasms, values and attitudes, even his very 'growing-points'. This raises all kinds of questions about the student experience. Can the academic teacher really communicate his enthusiasm for advancing knowledge? Is not the 'explosion of new knowledge' something that students just cannot cope with? Ought we not to stick to safe frameworks of examinable information and not attempt to move into the field of values? In any case, does not the gulf between the generations make the attempt to transmit any of our experience and culture a useless one? Thus, in this question of the transmission of knowledge, three different fields for discussion define themselves: the relation of research to teaching, the shape of curricula and examinations, the extent to which communication between the generations is possible in any but a very superficial sense.

The debate about research and teaching is a hot one. In the sciences particularly, it is said, the explosion of knowledge is so great that it must constitute an all-absorbing concern of some, whilst—well-removed from these eruptions—students are taught by others. The 'frontier position' is not one that students can really cope with: many are not exhilarated, but simply oppressed by the thought of an expanding universe of knowledge. Even research students feel the weight of this burden: it was a post-graduate student—in the humanities, not the sciences—who said: 'What will be the end-product of my work? Just one more article which poor, wretched students have to read.' Yet against this disillusionment we must set the deep conviction of many academics that teaching and research *must* fertilize each other. The advancement of knowledge, they say, cannot be separated from its transmission and the most vital thing to communicate is precisely enthusiasm for the ongoing process. Moreover, there is danger in allowing institutions of higher education to become wholly focused on a self-conscious process of transmitting knowledge. In a sense, transmission is always a by-product of the extension of knowledge and to let the two activities fall apart would be disastrous for both: our research institutions would become too professional, stream-lined and intensely focused on an esoteric activity, while undergraduate courses would tend to become stereotyped and unimaginative. It is notable that the Robbins Report has endorsed this instinctive belief in the mingling of teaching and research and—far from erecting barriers—has even suggested stepping-stones from undergraduate to research work, designed to make the approach to the frontier easier. Some trends today are certainly in the direction of more mingling: research is no longer confined chiefly to universities, but is being increasingly pursued in colleges of technology and education whose main activity is teaching. Thus the balance of opinion and present trends in this country endorse the view that higher education must be kept in close contact with the advancement of learning.

If this is accepted, however, we are still left with the problem of the over-burdened student. Even if we restrain ourselves from attempting to take him very near the frontiers of knowledge, the ever-increasing weight of what we must transmit is a huge problem in teaching and can be a most corrupting influence on methods of teaching. Particularly in the sciences, it is said, 'there is so much to communicate that it is necessary to spend a great deal of time just giving information; we are teaching twice as much as we ourselves had to learn'. 'This problem is worse at the university stage than in school; we do something which destroys imagination and self-expression in pushing in too much information.' For the teacher himself the struggle to organize and expound systematically the material he must give, to make it understood and to check that understanding, occupies an increasingly large amount of his time and energy. How can he, then, concern himself with the qualitative elements in his task—the training in critical judgment and perception of values about which we talk so much? Can he hope to create an atmosphere sufficiently relaxed for expansive conversation on the methods and significance of his subject, on his own particular enthusiasms and the problems he is trying to solve, on the whole philosophy of the subject? Finally, the sheer weight of information imposes itself on the examination system to such a degree that it is hard to break away from this tyranny. Yet the common assumption of examination papers that the only important thing is information, exercises a most deleterious influence over the whole student experience which tends to be governed by examination values. Students themselves are becoming increasingly restive under the burden of knowledge. A significant pointer today is the discussion of courses in student journals and the presentation by their committees of proposals to reform syllabuses.

Many academic teachers agree that there is a widespread intellectual *malaise* among students today. Its causes are complex and some of them we shall be discussing in a later chapter. The increasing burden of knowledge is certainly one and this is probably felt even more sharply to be an imposition because, precisely at a time when advancement of learning demands ever greater specialization, there is an instinctive move among students towards less specialization. Of course there are always some born specialists and others too timid or too lazy to want to look over walls or cross frontiers, but the striking feature today is the number of students of all levels of ability who want to do combined courses, or to hold 'frontier discussions' with other groups, or to pursue fringe studies or some form of art as well as their main course. This is perhaps a phenomenon of real significance, for may it not be the instinctive reassertion, in the midst of a gigantic departmentalization of life, of the need for wholeness in personal experience? One remembers the American student who said that the purpose of her college education was 'to round out her personality by broadening her background'. At any rate, the proliferation of new combined and experimental courses, in old universities as well as new, shows that the point is being taken.

But, it is argued, are we not giving students an inferior intellectual experience if we spread their courses too widely and do not bring them to understand in depth what knowledge really is? Here the debate is sharp, not only between teachers of different disciplines but even between those of the same. Thus some scientists claim that laboratory and book work could be cut down in order to give more time for getting perspective and seeing connections, whilst others argue that it is in the very nature of the present situation that sheer bulk of information will constrict courses more and more. 'It is not the explosion of knowledge that should be blamed,' says someone else, 'but our bemusement with it.' A good many people have a suspicion that it is lack of judgment and power of selection on the part of academic teachers that is the real cause of trouble. In a panic we try to stick to traditional frameworks while continually distending their bulk. We are too timid, it is said, too unsure of our academic standards and the validity of our authority. This is strikingly illustrated by the increased examination incubus precisely at a time when many begin to doubt its ability to test more than the ability to take examinations. 'Teachers are afraid of teaching without the examination incentive. They feel the lack of authority in our kind of society and therefore import it from the examination syllabus. There are many more courses in the university examination system than twenty years ago; we seem to be on the side of more examinations.' The question of cutting or extending courses and of how to test them are technical matters which can only be fought out in detail within the various disciplines, but it is worth asking, in general, what are the basic intellectual experiences which all students need?

From a number, we pick two for discussion. First, they need the experience of submitting their minds to discipline. Secondly, they need to find a core of personal meaning in their studies and to discover that this is illuminated by insights and connections from other parts of the general field of knowledge. But these two needs tend to lead us in opposite directions. Take discipline first. Nothing seems more important than that a student should submit his mind to the discipline of a chosen subject. The initial choice is his, but after that the discipline must be accepted. The subject itself imposes a structure and content and demands the acquisition of certain techniques. Choices within the framework are strictly limited and compulsory studies unavoidable. When we say 'the subject demands', we mean, of course, 'the specialists in charge of the subject demand', but the whole academic tradition of teaching in this country turns on the sense of responsibility which teachers have *towards their subject*. They are, as it were, the priests and priestesses of a mystery and no would-be acolyte is worth receiving unless he submits willingly to the discipline under which they themselves live. There is a kind of trinity of teacher, pupil and subject in which the third person is greatly important, even to the extent that the teacher will express anger at shoddy work because it is an insult to the subject. Thus syllabuses have always been determined more by the demands of the subject than the tastes of students, and it is taken for granted that reasonable proficiency in techniques must be achieved before much initiative can be enjoyed. As a form of education the value of this imposition of the austere requirements of a subject might seem to be beyond doubt, and yet there is great awareness that the second person of this trinity must be kept in full relationship to the other two. 'In teaching we must "kick" intellectually as hard as possible, but students must be made to realize that they are not being "kicked" *qua* persons. The social relations of teaching are vital if we are aiming to go intellectually as hard and as far as possible, because, unless we also convey personal concern, students think they are being got at. The teacher must show that, in engaging in research, he is himself undergoing this experience of being "kicked".' The focus on the student is carried even further in this remark: 'Our real concern should be to ask, not "What ought they to know?", but "What is it educationally valuable to teach?".'

Discipline is no good without a sense of personal meaning. 'Meaning' in this context is difficult to define because the worth of intellectual activity can grip the individual mind in so many different ways. It may be the sheer satisfaction of finding answers to questions or fitting pieces into puzzles; it may be the sense of illumination which highlights one's own living; it may be the quickening of imagination which enriches relations with others; it may be the realization of freedom to explore as your own mind dictates—there are a dozen ways in which to discover the meaning which makes intellectual discovery a personal possession. For the dedicated specialist the whole experience of a subject discipline is highly significant precisely because—though he may not know it—he has made a genuine personal commitment to that particular type of intellectual work. He has a built-in sense of meaning. But there are many young people today for whom 'meaning' has so far meant 'getting to college' and who, once they arrive are quite at sea about their purposes in acquiring knowledge. If their courses are conceived only in terms of external subject requirements, these will never become more than standard packets of information hung about their persons until examinations are over and then, maybe, flung away. Personal response to the values implicit in a subject, illumination as connections between diverse things suddenly appear, a sense of the meaning of truth in the inward parts—how are these to be made part of the average student's intellectual experience?

There must be varying answers to this question. We shall be arguing later that for some, at least, courses ought to be devised more from the viewpoint of their needs and interests than the demands of the subject discipline. For many there is surely a need to break away from traditional subject divisions and sub-divisions, to plan combined courses, cross-courses, comparative study courses, and, above all, to exercise discrimination in what we select as the essential body of information. Here some would stress the need for freedom from professional strait-jackets and the desirability of 'frontier-skirmishing' of various kinds. 'We are sometimes too bewitched by frontiers; what we are really concerned with in teaching is expanding the frontiers of the individual student. There is something to be said for amateurism, i.e. teaching something we don't know much about, because in the process we are together with the student. It is exhilarating together to see the horizon lift. The subject may be something well known to the specialist, but new to ourselves and the students.' 'Amateurism is not a heresy. I have always found it of great assistance to teach things I did not know well. At the same time, I believe we should be trying to carry students to the frontiers of knowledge.' For all, even the narrowest specialists, there is a crying need to examine 'meanings', both in terms of the significance of the subject and its methods for human living and in terms of value-problems which arise within it. Technical competence can never be a substitute for understanding. No one formula will do; always we have the two sides to balance in varying proportions: all students need an objective intellectual discipline, yet this remains sterile and externalized unless it acts upon a mind able and willing to take personal possession of the knowledge which it offers.

Thus we come back to the point that both learning and teaching are intensely personal activities. However objectively he selects and balances his material, no teacher can really communicate knowledge which is not a personal possession in that he regards it as significant and exciting, or at least as a stepping-stone to that which is significant and exciting. Learning, in the sense of the active reception of new knowledge, is equally personal. We are here, of course, excluding from 'education' the process by which a lecturer pre-packages information required in the examination market in a handy format and hands it across the counter to the students. The fundamental concern of higher education is with the authentic personal transmission and reception of knowledge, whether this takes place in lecture-room, laboratory, tutorial study or library, whether it is a transaction between one and many or one and few, whether contact is between the living, or between the living and the dead. At the heart of it all there are, or ought to be, personal relations.

This last statement at once impinges on our present concern with the vast new mass-movement into higher education. Are not personal relations ruled out automatically? Is there any real alternative to the 'pre-packaged' processing of the minds of students? This argument of despair assumes that 'personal relations' implies a predominance of small groups: the ideal image is that of the Oxford tutor with his feet on the mantelpiece, discussing an essay with one privileged student. But an equally valid image of 'personal communication' in higher education would be the eloquent and inspired lecturer holding a large audience under the spell of his discourse. The point is that a great deal of powerful personal communication can take place in large groups and this should be exploited to the full to meet the demands of expansion. All the devices of mass media can be brought into play to use on a large scale those who really can communicate themselves in this way.

Imparting knowledge in an organized discourse is one-half of the teaching job and there is little doubt that this can be done on a mass scale. But the other half of the task presents the real problem. The process of taking personal possession involves more than responding to a dynamic lecturer. It is hard to avoid the conclusion that every student must write fairly frequently and that every piece of writing must be discussed critically with a teacher. For one does not know what one possesses in the mind until trying to express it, and little progress in understanding can be made unless expressed thoughts are critically examined.

One of the strains most felt by first-year students, we are told, is the absence of the individual treatment which helped them through the Sixth Form phase: 'if they go to a university where there are no tutorials there can be great disappointment, because the sense of personal contact is lost and there is no impact of mind on mind'. Thus the case for the personal and fairly intimate academic relationship remains inescapable. It is the essential counterpart of the impact of personality in the large-scale lecture. If teacher-hours can be saved by the greater use of mass media in imparting information, they should be used in the small group, where assumptions can be examined, ideas pulled to pieces and a new synthesis built up.

But is there not a more fundamental problem? Are students today willing to receive from their teachers anything more than the information and techniques they need to start on their own path? Are we not deceiving ourselves in talking of the transmission of cultures and values, of enthusiasms and experience? Is there not in a new sense a 'war between the generations' today? Here there is much conflicting evidence and opinion. Some would say that the pace of change and the 'great divide' caused by World War II as well as the invention of nuclear weapons have created a situation between the generations which is qualitatively quite new. 'The students of the present generation were born during the war and the gap between them and us is to be accounted for by more than the passage of time; for them Hitler is a figure in a history book. They are further advanced in demanding, than we are in providing, an adjustment to an entirely new situation.' The autonomy of the present generation is seen in the growth of an independent youth culture which is seen as 'a real attempt to respond to its environment and to think through the problems of living—the kind of thing that is dealt with in the novels of Salinger and Golding and the theology of Tillich'. On the other side it is argued, first, that there is no more than the normal conflict between the generations today, and, secondly, that in any case a self-sufficient youth culture hardly exists in any but a most superficial sense. 'What is this youth culture? Certainly there is more minor initiative in relation to self-expression, but how far is this really a significant factor in student life? Does it represent anything more than the picking up of a few gimmicks?'

If 'war between the generations' really has been declared in any drastic sense, it cuts at the root of the transmission which, we have argued, is the central task of higher education. It raises, indeed, fundamental questions about culture and society. Why should we wish so strongly to transmit those values and truths we believe in? Should not each generation be free to create its own culture? What is the value of historical continuity in a society, except at the level of handing on know-how and useful information? But to pose the questions thus is at once to expose the absurdity of any notion of an absolute war between the generations. Whether they like it not, the next generation cannot help but build on our experience. They may repudiate it, but they cannot cut themselves off from it.

Probably we over-dramatize when we speak of 'war', but it serves as a necessary warning that we are not adjusting rapidly enough to a revolutionary situation. Academic institutions cannot abdicate from their historical role of making available the experience of the past to the present generation and this means that academic teachers must always be seeking to present past experience in ways that are currently relevant. Whether we attract or repel, the duty of trying to maintain or re-establish contact between the generations is inescapable. Perhaps, for all their assertions about the irrelevance of past experience, there is a cry for 'reconnection'. The complaints of first-year students cited above show their feeling of being cut off, and many small episodes reveal eagerness for re-establishing communication. There is a nice story of two youths who go round a roomful of contemporary pictures in a gallery, with all the appropriate exclamations of delight and comprehension, and then stray into a Constable room next door. Silence falls, until one says wistfully to the other: 'I *wish* I knew what he was trying to say to us!'

The great fear of the student experience is loneliness; the great desire is for relationships—with contemporaries certainly, and with teachers probably more than they will admit. In a certain sense, loneliness is inescapable: bookwork is a solitary pursuit and so is writing. The scientists come off better, since laboratory work, at least, can be a more social experience than library work. But most students find the strain of work that must be done in the solitude of their own minds very considerable. New student habits today show ingenious ways of studying in 'syndicates' and, above all, in twos. From one point of view we must see these as evasions of proper solitude, but we cannot help them to use solitude without fear unless we first see that they enjoy personal relations in their academic life. For the freedom to be solitary depends on a stable position in the community, and the hectic search for companionship often reveals how unsure of that they are. Solitariness and isolation are two quite different experiences. A true academic experience should mean a breaking out of isolation into a life of communication, with contemporaries and with teachers, with the living and the dead, with members of one's own society and with 'strangers' of many types. The great common task of all higher education could thus be described as the development of the power to understand and communicate with other human beings. Miss Glover discusses this task and some of its implications.

M. R.

Educating for Human Understanding

MARY GLOVER

I

The primary concern of all of us today must be with life as it has to be lived, and it is important to ask what society today needs that higher education can supply. There is no doubt at all that more scientists are needed and that higher education is helping to supply them. But with this I am not competent to deal. Again, there can be no question, there never has been any question, but that research in humane subjects—the work of a man like Sir Maurice Powicke, for instance—does throw light on human life, enlarging our understanding of the human predicament with a wider perspective and a deeper knowledge of the varieties and strength of human goodness, as well as the power and resources of self-seeking. Nevertheless, we do not need very many scholars of this kind: not every minister needs to read the Old Testament in Hebrew, but we do need a succession of Hebrew scholars to deepen our understanding of religion. Robbins's thousands are clearly not required for such work.

There is, however, a great range of human experience today where the need of understanding is tragically great and widespread and is not being met: this is the whole field of human relations. The root of this set of problems is the familiar simple fact of the difficulty of knowing, in face-to-face encounter, what the other person is experiencing. The failure to perceive this creates resistant difficulties in politics, in international relations, in the clash of colour; in the hostility and strikes that bedevil industry; in the bewilderment of society in dealing with the delinquent, or of anybody in dealing with the young; even in relations between man and wife. In all these situations human selfishness is powerfully at work, but they are exacerbated by failure of understanding. It is commonly assumed that nothing but intuition will overcome this difficulty and this gift is rare. Some people mistake quick reaction for it. But in the twentieth century, as never before, this failure of understanding can be much lessened by training. Has higher education an obligation of response to this need? I think it has.

The universities have for a long time been making a contribution to human understanding, traditionally through the humanities and the way they have been taught. In history and literature, in the classics and in other languages, it is possible to focus upon the realities of human experience, including, when the documents permit this, the intimate private experience of individual minds. Somebody has commented on how fine a thing it was that the first factory inspectors, appointed in 1833, were men with university degrees 'who had read Euripides'. I am not sure that today even a classical scholar would appreciate the relevance of Euripides to factory inspection. But it is indubitable. Euripides always perceives, and relentlessly compels his readers to perceive, what it is like to be the underdog, the slave, the captive of war, the woman, the foreigner. And the factory inspectors' reports reveal that they *were* perceptive in this way, sensitive to the difficulties of factory employees as well as employers, of factory children and their parents, of factory doctors and teachers, even the stoker trying to teach grimy children to read from grimy primers in the coal-hole.

But today this human concern has been pretty well driven out of classical and humane studies by the overpowering interest in philology and literary form. Today people who have had a classical education are apt to say either that it trains you in exactness, or that it is useless, never that it helps one to understand human life more perceptively.

The de-humanizing of humane studies has, in fact, already been partly compensated by the acceptance of the social sciences—of psychology, politics, international relations, economics, sociology—as courses in higher education. Some have been accepted for years, and the newer universities are greatly interested in them. Psychology would appear to be pre-eminently a discipline which could be combined with fruitful results in a two-subject honours course, e.g. with literature or history. There could come a cross-fertilization of types of learning that might lead to a far more sensitive perception of what happens to human beings in the situations which are studied in history and literature.

Among the social sciences there is a great need for the development of training for management. In all sorts of places—hospitals, schools, offices, factories, colleges, universities—one finds that unhappiness and frustration are chronic, simply because those whose business it is to manage other people cannot do it with proper awareness and skill. This damages the quality of the work people are able to do. Of the economic consequences of bad management I am not competent to speak; I do, however, remember a responsible official working for the Coal Board saying that in some pits 'human relations were worth 37s. 6d. a ton'. There is a good deal of evidence that many people in management do not know what their people are feeling, nor how they interpret what management says and does.

There seems, however, to be a danger in the social sciences at present of exclusive attention to facts for which statistical evidence can be obtained. There is obviously great need for statistical inquiry, but it is not true that what cannot be counted is of no significance. There are some facts that can only be learnt in face-to-face encounter, and if in such encounter one is blind, insight will not be achieved at all: all that statistics can do is to accumulate unintelligible facts. For instance, it is possible to count the number of old people living in institutions: it takes sensitive face-to-face encounter to find out, as Peter Townsend did, that institutional life commonly entails, amongst other deprivations, 'loneliness, loss of privacy and identity, and collapse of powers of self-determination'.[1] In fact, the immense prestige of science can be a threat to the integrity and meaning not only of social studies but also of social training. A case in point was given by Dr. Walk in a recent number of the *Journal of Mental Science*.[2] He records how a noble tradition of mental nursing was built up by the Quakers at the Retreat at York from 1797, based chiefly on sensitive attention to the patient. He shows that about a hundred years later this tradition was 'obscured', because mental nurses wanted the same prestige as hospital nurses and accordingly developed a training of hospital type. But hospital nurses were themselves coveting the prestige of medical students and loading their courses heavily with scientific subjects, especially anatomy and physiology. Medical courses were themselves, perhaps, over-influenced by the magnetic prestige of science.

Social sciences can be defended against this kind of impoverishment by two forces; one of these is literature. It is the poets and novelists who compel us to experience, under the skin, the things that happen to other people—as Euripides has done. It seems a pity for social studies to develop without the benefit of literature. The second truly humanizing force is vocational training, especially training for teaching and social work. Both these involve a focus on the individual and his experience. They do much to overcome the failure of natural intuition in face-to-face encounter, and thus to enlarge our potential range of human understanding. This is achieved in two main ways: first, psychology adds to our knowledge of the structure of personality and the common reactions to stress; secondly, training teaches an attitude of mind in the learner which enables him to offer respect and warmth of response to someone who is in danger of alienating the sympathy of those who have to do with him, yet can only be helped by meeting with respect and friendly support.

Common sense does not suffice to enable us to deal wisely with people who are behaving unreasonably. 'I just can't understand why he should behave like that' is the signature-tune of common sense, *vis-à-vis* people who cannot behave properly because their own minds are in a tangle which they cannot understand. Such people—and children too—are often unable to help themselves by verbalizing their feelings. A man coming to a social agency for assistance is perhaps unable to say: 'It humiliates me to be here asking for help,' but his *malaise* may express itself in rudeness. The trained worker can interpret behaviour which baffles mere common sense. As one case-worker said: 'There is a look of relief and astonishment that comes over the face of the client, when you have put into words something which has long been a trouble to him, but which he could not recognize nor find the words for himself.' Such understanding is itself healing and it is often the fruit, not of uninstructed intuition, but of good training.

In spite of the fact that such training commands small esteem in academic circles, and is in danger of distortion from the prestige of other disciplines, it is important to have such teachers and such students in the academic community, chiefly because of the influence students exercise on students. A brilliant young graduate physicist said to me, that one of the things he most hoped to learn from his fiancée, a social work student, was her understanding of people. Social work students are also valuable because of their sense of purpose. This is not a vague idealism: they get a realistic awareness of the actual conditions in which their work will lie from their practical training periods, and in the student community they help to assuage the sense of living in a world which students constantly call 'unreal'—the ivory tower.

II

One of the big questions which faces universities in a time of expansion is the matter of teaching. Is it necessary to *teach* at all, in the sense of individual teaching as distinct from lecturing? The ablest people teach themselves, whatever their teachers do. At the other end of the scale, it has been abundantly proved that many students can get degrees on lectures and reading-lists and examinations. A university education should at least teach one to work responsibly on one's own, with the help of books.

It is perhaps waste of time for a fine scholar, engrossed in research, to be obliged to give tutorial time to students who are not interested in scholarship and who regard the tutorial either as a bore or as a way of getting the tutor to do the work they will not do for themselves. In fact, the easiest way of taking some tutorials is to comply with this expectation and engage in monologue, because the students cannot rise to dialogue. But such monologue is really waste of time; if one was going to talk so much, with so much care and learning, one should have lectured to a larger number. It is true that some fine scholars are able to inspire some very unlikely students, at least temporarily, to a real interest in their studies. But I do not think there are many who can do this, nor many unintellectual students who can respond generously to such an effort.

Nevertheless, there are cogent reasons for offering tutorial teaching to students who show themselves capable of enjoying and responding to such teaching. One reason is related to the experience students are getting during their academic course. Between the ages of eighteen and twenty-two there is tremendous development of character: people are revising and strengthening their attitudes to life in a very different mood from that of the uncertain younger teenager. What academic courses seem generally to secure is that during these sensitive, dynamic years the younger generation are pretty well confined to the company of their own age-group. Their age-group is supremely important to them. Yet the strength of human civilizations has largely lain in the ability of the older generation to pass on to the younger the fruits of experience and tradition. Today, if the student does have much contact with older people—his family or his landlord —it is apt to be with seniors who have little understanding of the student experience nor sympathy with it.

In part this situation, in which the Senior Common-Room and the Union live side by side with little effective communication, is created by the tendency of young people to hold off from their seniors. They think older people want to dominate them, but lack the fundamental wisdom that would justify them in doing so. In short, they tend to think the older generation has little to offer. We do seem often to be in a muddle, unable to expound a coherent philosophy about such matters as religion, politics or sex, and out of touch with the realities of student life at the university and at home. The young, on the other hand, are confident. The broadcast by Dennis Chapman[3] on *The Autonomous Generation* gave, I think, a fair picture of them. One senses immense vigour in the student group: they are not at all the passive recipients of what we may have to bestow. They are making their own attitudes to life, accepting the strain of the twentieth century with courage. They make mistakes and sometimes come literally to grief, but they have very strong ethical principles, which they have not accepted on authority but seem to have worked out for themselves as fresh assessments of human obligation. I think they often find their academic teachers selfish and competitive and far from charitable to each other; students are often noticeably kind and concerned for one another. They honour equality and abhor privilege and have a compassion which is impressive. This finds an outlet in work camps and other social work, as well as in their sense of obligation to their families and friends. In this we must not forget that the family relations of students in the present generation are difficult beyond all precedent, since they are so often the first in the family history to have a higher education.

In spite of the hiatus between the generations and the self-confidence of the young, it is the case that many students would like more contact with staff on more human terms. The staff would often like it too. It seems waste of opportunity to spend one's years in constant contact with young people and not to get to know them well. There are difficulties in making social contacts, arising partly from changing modes of hospitality. In my young days dons would invite students to Sunday breakfast (the porter brought up a tray of bacon and eggs, and the ration of eggs per person was five); or in large droves to Sunday tea in their homes; or *à deux* to walk round the Parks (in Cambridge to do the Grantchester Grind). Students today do not enjoy that kind of hospitality. They have not the gift of small talk—often not of highbrow talk either—and they do not know when to go. They do not walk. The clue to this difficulty is the casual meeting on neutral ground: there is great need for bars and common-rooms where staff and students can meet casually and without protocol. Students sometimes are accused of 'creeping' if they are known to go often to a staff house, except for baby-sitting.

But the most effective means of getting to know students is through tutorial teaching, and the justification for spending time in this way is that, when tutorials go well, they are rewarding to both teachers and taught. It is through individual teaching—a tutor with one, two or three students—that the impact of character on character is most felt, that the student discovers value in the traditions of scholarship, of courtesy and respect for persons, of truthfulness and humility in thought, while the older person is able to make effective contact with the younger, to sense his response to problems, and the special quality of a young mind at grips with life. This type of teaching depends on perceiving what is going on in a student's mind, what experience he is actually having of his subject, where his difficulties come up, where the trend of his interest is going, where his real gifts come into operation and can be supported.

It may be objected that all students do not wish to have their minds penetrated and guided in this way, that it may be regarded as an intrusion on their privacy or autonomy. One is reminded of the comment made by a French social-worker after a year spent on a case-work course in America: 'Yes, but it is terrible to be so deeply understood.' The answer to this is that a sensitive teacher should know when a student wishes to be let alone.

Mary Glover

Individual teaching, springing from a genuine involvement in the student's learning experience and concern for his individual development as a thinker and scholar, makes a deep impression on the learner. It can remain with him as a basic concept in all personal relations and even carry over into his relations with employees, children, colleagues. Not that he has to teach all these people, but that he has accepted the idea that the right way of dealing with them springs from a sensitiveness to them and to the experience they are having. This kind of sensibility, once learnt, seems to be transferable, and it is here that a major contribution of higher education can be made to the great problem of human relations.

This kind of teaching, however, is very difficult to supply, for a number of reasons. People with much ability to concern themselves with students, and to make of teaching a sensitive and generous personal relationship, are not apparently very numerous. A proportion of them feel drawn to school-teaching, and I think some students sense the difference between Sixth-Form teaching which has this personal quality and university instruction which often has not. It is relevant to recognize that Sixth-Form teaching is focused on success in immediate examinations and the success is accredited to the teacher as well as the learner. In the universities there is much less tendency to judge a teacher by the examination successes of his pupils, so that the reward for good and devoted teaching is not an enhancement of one's own standing; in fact good teaching brings very little external reward. The rewards in terms of enhanced standing, promotion and higher pay are channelled to research. Thus the academic teacher, who can teach well and wishes to, is under the strain of knowing that unless he pushes forward with publishable research quickly, he will be left behind. He knows, moreover, that promotion can have a quite noticeable effect on his family life, indeed, may even affect the number of children he and his wife feel it right to have.

If all who can teach well, and wish to do so, had both time and incentives for it, there would still not be enough good teachers for greatly increased numbers. Good teachers are generally ready to overwork themselves and are apparently to be required to do so. But to overwork a good teacher is a sure way of making him go stale. This penalizes both sides. It is a cruel thing to do to teachers, since it tends to destroy the very thing that should be the source of their joy in their work—the energy and originality of their own minds. This can be a traumatic experience.

The only answer to this that I can see is to release time by using 'canned' lectures and the 'university of the air'. This should make it possible to get much better lectures as a usual thing and to make the burden of tutorial work much more supportable. Students who are to receive tutorial teaching should be selected on the basis of the work they have done and the promise they show of being able to profit from it and enjoy it. Or if, in some subjects, teachers feel it important to give all first-year students tutorials, in order at the outset to show them the lines on which they are to work, it still need not follow that in every year every student should have this privilege. Tutorial resources are of the greatest value and must be husbanded carefully.

What is higher education for? My own tentative answer would be that its purpose is to understand the needs of the community today and help to meet them. These needs include scientific and social research and teaching, especially research and teaching in the whole field of human relationships. Humane and social studies form an important part of this. The years spent by young people in higher education put upon universities and colleges a responsibility for helping them as persons at a time of rapid and formative personal growth. They need first the illuminating experience of being understood themselves, and then the second illuminating experience of finding out how they can begin to get inside the thoughts and emotions of all sorts and conditions of men. They need this experience both for its own intrinsic meaning to themselves and because of its transferability into the future texture of their relationships. They can receive it partly through the content of their study courses, partly through the methods by which they are taught and partly through the provision of enjoyable opportunities for casual meetings with senior people. What they can afterwards do with this understanding in society is immeasurable.

NOTES

1. P. Townsend, *The Last Refuge* (London, 1962), p. 434.
2. A. Walk, 'The History of Mental Nursing', *Journal of Mental Science* 107 (1961), pp. 1–17.
3. D. Chapman, 'The Autonomous Generation', *The Listener*, 17th January 1963.

Part Three

EXPANSION
AND DIVERSIFICATION IN
HIGHER EDUCATION

The terms of reference under which what we call the Robbins Committee was set up struck a new note in its commission to consider Higher Education as one whole, and the Robbins Report has made an important contribution to the establishment of this way of thinking. This, as we have already argued, is the right way to view it today, bearing in mind the common experiences and responsibilities of all students in full-time (or equivalent) education for at least three years beyond the age of eighteen. It is notable that the call to expansion in the Robbins Report is made chiefly on grounds of educational justice *to the age-group*. From the 'bulge' (the actual increase in the size of the age-group) to the 'trend' (the increasing proportion of the age-group demanding places), the figures lead inexorably to the conclusion that 'by 1980 this country should be providing entry to full-time higher education for about 17 per cent of the age-group' (p. 66). The setting of the whole argument is a sociological one. Better nurture means more ability to profit by education, especially at the upper level. The longer parents stay in education themselves, the more they will demand higher education for their children. National prosperity encourages investment in long-term training with a view to better careers and a higher standard of living at the end. The rewards for higher skills are rising. So also is the social esteem in which higher education is held. All the forces of parental ambition, school influence and economic opportunity are pressing boys and girls to stay longer at school: appetite increases with consumption and therefore, more having qualified, more will want to go on to college. Thus the convergence of social factors is built up, but the basic conception underlying this case is one of justice to the individual—the claim that every young person should be equipped to make as full a response as possible (commensurate with his ability) to his environment. Furthermore, it is because 'education ministers intimately to ultimate ends, in developing man's capacity to understand, to contemplate

123

and to create' that therefore 'where there is capacity . . . there that capacity should be fostered' (p. 8).

This is an undeniable plea for justice in education. It underscores a significant fact of human experience—that frustrations develop in proportion to expanding possibilities, since opportunity hardly ever keeps pace with possibility. What is seen today as an urgent matter of social justice could not conceivably have been thought of in this way a hundred years ago. But it is only too apparent to all those engaged in the struggle to meet this new demand for justice that there are crying dangers in the whole process of expansion. What is happening to the essential student experience? What kind of farcical justice is it if we line them all up and hand out stones for counterfeit bread? The dangers are obvious and have been eloquently stated by Dr. Wilson. The point we wish to make is that they are common to all kinds of institutions. If real social justice is to be done, we must not slip into the error of a double standard, making a desperate attempt to preserve for some the more favourable conditions of education, whilst content that the many should be mass-processed in various ways. A true student experience is the right of all students in all universities and colleges. Yet, as Professor Niblett points out in the following essay, the traditional image of student life in the public mind is drawn from the ancient universities and was thought of originally as belonging to a small *élite*. This image has, of course, been in process of change for some time and under the impact of expansion the metamorphosis is speeding up. Yet is it not important, in moving forward into this great new phase of expansion, to preserve and adapt some of our traditional values? Dr. Wilson argues that they must be preserved at all costs. We have to look searchingly at possible 'costs', both of expansion and preservation. Many would agree that the cost of expansion is too high if it means providing a spurious substitute experience for all. But equally many would say that the cost of preservation is too high if it means a 'double standard' in higher education. Whether the process be termed 'adaptation' or 'dilution', traditional values must undergo modification to meet the needs of expansion. Professor Niblett discusses the direction in which the Robbins Report is pushing us with this problem in mind.

M.R.

Expansion and Traditional Values

W. R. NIBLETT

A school or university is more dependent than it often realizes upon what the public expects from it. For the image it fills in the national mind will affect both the attitude of students who enter it and of the men and women who teach in it. Some of the achievements and non-achievements of our public schools, for example, depend upon the respect and the status we allow them in our society; some of the ineffectiveness of certain of our secondary modern schools is due to the respect we deny them.

Now to the majority of English men and women—of very diverse incomes and social backgrounds—the word university still brings Oxford and Cambridge first to mind. Most ordinary people think of a university even in 1963 as a place for a small, socially selected, and clever minority. It is a privilege for them to be there. They are licensed during term time to be more leisured than most young people of their age and they will have far longer vacations than the majority, holidays they can use more or less as they like. In the last twenty-five years—since the war—the idea of universities as places for a scientific education and for scientific research has begun to get home. Even in the mind of the man in the street nuclear physics has become a 'U' subject. But the Oxbridge ideal of what a university should be still understandably has great power not only with him but also among those with knowledge and influence, including many heads of grammar schools. And they see it far more clearly than he does as a place to which you belong rather than one you attend, which has a power within the whole mind and not only within the intelligence, where, though the young may sing tenor freely, there is a bass accompaniment from their seniors which adds much to the completeness and civilization of the tune. It is significant that among the most desirable Red-bricks, at least for the study of the arts, the ones still highest in the league tables of applicants from many good schools are those thought to be in one way or another most like Oxbridge— Bristol and St. Andrews, Durham, Exeter, some of the London colleges. The image which Keele and Sussex and now York are establishing, not without advertising skill, is a pretty Oxbridge one. But is there not a lot to be said for this?

Into this situation comes Robbins bringing its own special brand of light. It says fresh things, but also, more powerfully than we have ever heard, some of the things which the U.G.C. and various Government reports had said more feebly already. The Report shows clearly that universities are needed by the nation for technological, scientific, business and professional studies on a much bigger scale than before. They are indispensably useful: and so, though there must be no lowering of academic standards, there must be an enormous increase in the total number of students going to them. The majority of this extra provision must be in the big cities, in universities that are large compared with what we have been accustomed to. All this must have its effect upon the public image of a university. Even if public expectation has changed in certain respects, Robbins has given it a further mighty push in the direction in which it was already tending to go. And yet the Robbins Committee was conscious of the permanent importance of the older image too: its Report is anxious not only that social justice shall be done to the intelligent young man or woman by providing him with higher education but that that education shall nourish him.

The recommendations are for more than a threefold increase in student numbers in the nineteen years 1961–80. By the latter date there should be more members of university staff in this island than there were students thirty-five years ago—350,000 students then as compared with 113,000 in 1961. But the greatest increase must be in the proportion of technologists—something like a fivefold multiplication between 1961 and 1980. At least ten Colleges of Advanced Technology will henceforward be universities—and not just reckoned as universities but accepted as such. Presumably the heads of each of the S.I.S.T.E.R.S., of all the ten C.A.T.s and several of the universities will themselves be technologists. By 1980 in most of the greater cities of

England there will be large and conspicuous new buildings in use for university purposes. Several towns will have more than one university, each with its post-graduate schools: already Glasgow is in that position, shortly Manchester and London will be, soon perhaps Birmingham, maybe Bristol. It will become more and more obvious that a university education is desirable, if not indispensable, for many posts which up to now have not demanded it, not only jobs in industry but, for example, in local government, transport administration, stock-broking, the social services—and even shipbuilding, which has kept itself fairly unspotted so far.

But can we give a really central, personal education to so much larger a number of university students, some of whom will probably be part-time students anyway? It could come about, despite the Robbins hopes, that the universities are looked to primarily for the production of large numbers of technically trained, normal, sensible, people, who fit in with normal society, who see ideas simply as tools, to whom the notion of a 'play of ideas' will be quite alien.

Foreseeing such things, the Report has argued the need for (i) a continued high ratio of university staffing as compared with most countries; (ii) greater attention to teaching ability—which is always a very personal affair—in lecturers; (iii) staff-student contacts to be made easy; (iv) an evolution in the pattern of much degree work so that the dangers of an inhumane type of specialization should be reduced. In maintaining this it is without doubt expressing not only the opinion of its members but also that of informed opinion generally. That is one of the strengths of Robbins: it is so representative a document. All the same, one wonders whether the safeguards proposed will be enough. Will most universities in the future be instruments of general education of the same potency as some at any rate have been in the past? Not that all have been particularly potent in this regard. I remember, still, visiting twenty-five years ago the dreary town of Billingham in County Durham with its great I.C.I. factories and their research departments, in which I was told 424 graduate chemists and physicists were then employed, most of whom lived near at hand. The difficulties of getting any cultural activities at all to go on in the place were tremendous. Nobody was interested or felt responsible.

Whenever changes are made in function and therefore in

structure within great institutions one must look for far-reaching, not altogether prophesiable, consequences. No institution ever works entirely according to conscious intention and least of all one into which new elements and purposes have deliberately been incorporated. May the danger not be, in spite of Robbins safeguards, for future students to be less in real touch with their teachers than now? What image of their own possibilities and of the nature of man will students be given? How highly will universities value not only the knowledge and skills they specifically teach but reflectiveness, insight into other people's moods and motives, capacity for moral judgment, and so on? In its discreet way the Report says that it is the duty of universities to ensure that subjects that are 'important' but that do not attract great numbers of students are 'adequately' studied. But what is the criterion of 'important' and of 'adequately'? How important, for example, are not merely Hindustani and Far Eastern History, but Philosophy, Theology, Metaphysics, Ethics, Music and Fine Art? We are told (page 149) that different patterns of education would have different effects upon the national economy. But they will of course have potent effects, too, upon other facets of national and personal life than the economic. The Robbins Committee saw that but did they reckon sufficiently with the utilitarian outlook that a technological society itself may produce?

The fact is that hidden within such terms as 'the nation's needs', 'if manpower is not to be wasted', 'a proper balance between teaching and research', 'the well-being of further education', the maintenance by this densely populated island of 'an adequate position in the fiercest competitive world of the future', are value-judgments. It was not the business of the Robbins Committee to look very closely into them: its concern was with the future pattern of higher education, not with an analysis of the values influencing the creation of that pattern.

But if universities are instruments of education their objectives and built-in, maybe subconscious, evaluations are immensely important. It is illuminating in this regard to look more carefully at the chapter in Robbins on Aims and Principles—as carefully written as any. In it the objectives of higher education are set out in a very contemporary—and discussable—way. Briefly they are defined like this:

- (*a*) The first, which is specifically declared to be not the

most important, is to educate skills of a practical and vocational kind. This aim, it is declared, has been undervalued
in the recent past—we must not undervalue it in future.

(*b*) The second principle is to promote what are called 'the
general powers of the mind'; the aim being to produce 'cultivated' men and women. But almost immediately this is
glossed by a suggestion that such general education will enable those who receive it to apply their minds to *problems*.
'It is this', the Report declares, 'that the world of affairs
demands of the world of learning.' And later on the essential
business of a first-degree course is defined as teaching the
student 'how to think' (page 90). In other words the interpretation of what 'cultivated' means is fairly intellectual.

(*c*) Thirdly, a university education is defined as concerned
with the advancement of learning and what is called 'the
search for truth'—truth perhaps being understood as more
likely to be discovered by our going out to find it than by
learning what life itself has to teach if one can accept it.

(*d*) The fourth purpose is described as 'the transmission of
a common culture and common standards of citizenship'. The
slight vagueness of this—unusual in Robbins—seems to indicate the difficulty members had in saying exactly what was
meant. But the sentences which follow do help to elucidate
the meaning somewhat. 'We believe', they say (though the
verb indicates a certain tentativeness), 'that it is a proper
function of higher education, as of education in schools, to
provide in partnership with the family that background of
culture and social habit upon which a healthy society depends.' I do not quite know what partnership with the family
involves and there is little in the Report to suggest how the
family connection is to be fostered. But certainly it is implied
that a university as a society is to provide standards of honesty,
good taste and fair dealing which will have a lasting influence
upon its members.

(*e*) Finally, in a summary a little later in the chapter, the
Report vindicates higher education for all those qualified to
take it on two main grounds: that more of it will enable
Britain to compete better with other economically developed
countries, and that such education 'ministers intimately to
ultimate ends by developing man's capacity to understand,
to contemplate and to create', thus giving a chance to intelli-

I   129

gent citizens 'to become not merely good producers but also good men and women'.

In spite of this latter phrase it can fairly be said that the Robbins recommendations as a whole stress the development of rationality rather than the kind of understanding that involves feeling, of an active and directed intelligence rather than a contemplative, and that they emphasize our economic expectations from this tremendous investment of money in brain-power in higher education rather than a fostering of creativeness, except of an inventive and applied type. And yet, no right reading of the Report would suggest that this is the whole intention. Its fabric is shot silk. In its concern for equal reward for equal work for what it calls 'high excellence', and the significance it gives to communication between teachers and taught and to community life in the university, it is a very humane document. It never for one moment thinks of students or staff as 'brains on stilts'. Nevertheless one does wonder if the full range of depersonalizing influences coming from outside the universities upon the students of 1970 or 1980 has been adequately reckoned with. Are these universities of the future going to have all the power *within* their students that is called for? Are they going to be more interested in educating their students than most Red brick universities are in 1963?

For Sir Charles Morris is surely right in thinking that universities today are not willing to concern themselves much with the really basic problems of education.[1] Up to now most Red brick university departments have been most interested in producing academics, though the word of course must be interpreted in a liberal sense. Morris contends that today it is the pure scientists, especially the physicists and chemists, who are the effective guardians of the conscience of universities. And how true, by and large, that is anyone who knows a Red brick university will testify. By 1980 pure scientists may well be in even greater positions of power relative to arts people than now, though by that time the social scientists and engineers will have come further into the picture. One certainly has cause for doubting, however, if most university teachers will be as concerned about the education of their students as all-round men and women as Robbins would like.

What then is to be done? If the universities are to develop as instruments of education as well as research, I suggest that more attention will have to be given to such points as these:

First, the motivation for the provision of more tertiary education as well as better secondary and primary education ought to be less the appeal to material national needs, and more than perhaps it is, the need both of individuals and nations to improve their quality of life. Maybe indeed that is what civilization is about, though we are shy of saying so. What else is it for anyway?

Secondly, if we are to be more successful in giving general education, a more perceptive and perhaps humbler approach is needed to the teaching of facts. The sheer unreasonableness of facts is so little emphasized or even seen. Facts, rocky realities as Galbraith the economist has called them, are often so unexpected. Whoever would regard human birth as a reasonable way of coming into the world? Or have thought up the process of swallowing through the mouth as a reasonable way of keeping alive? The body, the ebb and flow of the sea waves, Kant's moral law within, have to be accepted on experience as facts— and not without humility. A real acceptance of facts can never be a textbook affair but an acceptance of evidence—and against all the probabilities more often than we allow.

Thirdly, it is important to provide for the exercise of reasoning ability outside as well as inside a specialism. In this respect as well as others the programme of studies at several of the newest universities seems promising. Sussex, Essex and East Anglia have, of course, neatly and deliberately got rid of their Faculties of Arts altogether, and with them the tendency of such Faculties to be over-conservative. The Schools of European Studies and Social Studies or Comparative Studies they have set up or are proposing may yield, with luck, a number of not too usual exercises in thought and reasoning across subject barriers. A meditative comparison of the legal or governmental systems of France and England; or of the economic history of Great Britain and Italy; or the literatures of England and Spain can, if properly conducted, offer real scope to thought. But without doubt the less able the student the more planned must the help be which is offered to him if he is really to give his mind to problems outside the hedges of the fields to which his forthcoming examination may appear naturally to confine him.

And that brings me to my fourth point. 'Giving his mind,' I said. For many people really giving the mind to something requires an example. They work best either if they become members of a group whose interest is warm and kindling or under the individual lead of somebody they trust. Enthusiasm is an immensely valuable quality in teachers, including university teachers. It is the link with youth. Too little investigation has been done of how a team of research workers in science gets its results, of the ways in which the contributions made by each member of the unit helps forward the work. It is not a matter of thinking only, important though that is, but of knowing to whom you can turn, of the insertion at the appropriate stage of humour, or a spot of praise, or a question, so that the group-spirit is kept almost from minute to minute at the right temperature and at the right distance from its objective. Scientific study is educative not only to the logical abilities, but at any rate in the laboratory to intuition and judgment and some forms of sympathy. But it is most likely to be so if a lead is given—not necessarily by a Rutherford or a Hardy but by a lecturer who is liked or respected, or even by a fellow student.

More research is needed into the ways in which groups function. Such research might indeed benefit university education, or at least university teaching, very considerably—which is more, I think, than can really be said for a good deal of the research which is supposed almost automatically to make the university teacher into, not merely a better teacher, but a better man, a pleasant supposition which does really cry aloud for a good deal more evidence than is usually vouchsafed.

A university which is to be an instrument of education needs to be varied and human in its encouragements—not a society of 'committed cold fish'. The bigger universities grow and the less collegiate they are, the more necessary it may be for the student to be in fairly close touch with at least one of his seniors. We have really done quite remarkably little thinking about counselling and guidance so far in Red brick universities, at any rate outside the departments themselves. There is a little more for women, in some universities, than for men through the Tutor for Women Students whose functions in several are to give academic advice as well as personal. The more 'offerings', as the American call them, that are available, the more guidance and re-guidance facilities are also likely to be necessary. The best counsellors understand not merely the requirements but the needs of their students. In fact, the more planned the overall curriculum of a university, the more planned must its advisory services be. We have much to learn about the printed and illustrated information we make available on our universities and their courses—though these have improved considerably in recent years. But we have more still to learn about how to guide the student around, in a really big and complex set-up, to the programmes and courses that will help him most as an individual.

Universities could perhaps more often learn some of the things I have referred to from their Departments of Education and indeed their Training Colleges than from most places. This is one reason among several why it is important if Schools of Education come into being, as I hope they will, that they should remain in intimate touch with the whole university. There is a possibility that they may not. They may become a good deal more separated from their university as a whole even than most Medical Schools—large communities with their own administrative set-up and far too little influence on the university. This is certainly not what Robbins intends. But it may happen.

Finally, for some students and members of staff services or meetings held at an appropriate religious centre within the university can do much to give meaning and purpose to their studies. It is remarkable how little is ever said about the contribution in a university which a chapel can make to the fulfilment of minds and lives.

What I have in fact been saying is that universities in the future should be trying to do in a different context very much what the Oxbridge collegiate and tutorial system at its best sought to do with very small numbers of students in an age which has now largely vanished. That system did its stuff without much planning and without much conscious 'educational theory'. Indeed those very words were like a knell. But in a post-Robbins era this will not do. One has now deliberately to dig up all sorts of good but buried presuppositions if they are not to be lost without trace.

The public image must be retained that a university is a society of free men and women concerned with studies that are of permanent, not only instrumental, value; and the universities must be encouraged to see more clearly their function as places of education in depth as well as width. The dangers to individuality and personality which the next two decades may bring with them must not be underestimated. Against them the universities are among our chief bastions.

NOTE

1. Cf. *The Expanding University* (Faber and Faber, 1962), p. 19.

One of the aspects of expansion to which the Robbins Committee perhaps paid too little attention is the need for bolder diversity in courses which should rank roughly equal in parity of esteem. If the best of our traditions in academic life are to be spread through a much more varied range of students, we shall have to embody them in many non-traditional shapes. That the category 'student' will embrace a greater range of ability, outlook and motive seems certain. The Robbins Committee drew a firm ability line based on the qualification of two 'A' levels, but most people agree that this places above the line many who have neither the ability nor the motive-force to pursue an orthodox honours course fruitfully. Perhaps it is the depth of the 'pool of motive' which we doubt even more than that of the 'pool of ability'. Watered-down versions of courses traditionally structured for the few will not fulfil the kind of educational justice we are seeking; academic values must be translated into bold new experiments. It is here that the Robbins Committee seemed too timid, tailoring their suggestions for new types of course too closely to university models and showing too much concern for 'maintaining standards'. Nobody quite knows, of course, what present academic standards are and it could not be maintained that they never fluctuate. Many academic teachers, however, are clear that the ability line of two 'A' levels is no guarantee that even the varying degree-standards of the present can or ought to be maintained. We should get a much better grasp of our educational purpose if we abandoned deceptive talk about maintaining standards and looked at the question the other way round. The real claim being made is not that all those with two 'A' levels can maintain present standards, but that all these—if they wish for it—can profit by some form of higher education. Standards must be shaped to the people rather than the people to the standards. If we accept this proposition, we can proceed to build up the right kind of courses with freedom, instead of trying to fit all-comers to various existing sizes of Honours, General or Pass

135

Procrustean beds. A certain basic standard is already established in the qualification for entry and above this the only solution to greatly varying educational needs is great diversity in the conception of courses.

The range of motive and interest is as crucial as the range of ability. Generally speaking, there are three types of approach to higher education: the specialist interest in a subject, the broadly cultural interest and the vocational. The first is, of course, traditionally catered for in the honours course which may often need reforming but does not raise problems of new approaches and standards. A great many of the students of the new expansion come into the second category. Miss Glover describes the outlook and needs of some of these:

'What of the thousands who "qualify" for entrance by getting two passes at "A" level, who are not at present admitted to universities but will be coming into higher education in the future?

'I feel I have met these people in later life and know something of their needs. In Extra-Mural work I have taught Youth Employment Officers, National Assistance Officers, Child Care Officers, nurses, midwives and others in skilled and responsible jobs. Many of them would, in my judgment, have achieved two "A" levels, if they had the chance, and all of them had a keen desire for knowledge. Their experience in their jobs had made them want to know more about the background and implications of what they were doing: they wanted history, psychology, sociology, literature. And I think they were right: further education in these subjects would really have enabled them to do their work, not with more devotion, but with a more enlightened perspective, a surer sense of direction and more human understanding. Also, I think, with more pleasure, and I cannot forget one of the things Aristotle said about pleasure (a subject to which he recurred several times), namely, that pleasure in doing anything *perfects the activity*.

'Nevertheless, if they were brought into a university to take honours courses in these subjects, still more if they had been brought in before they had experience in their jobs, I think their motivation would have faltered. They were interested in literature because literature throws light on human nature, but I think Beowulf, or even the Fair Field Full of Folk, would have seemed to them irrelevant; they were interested in psychology, but experiments on rats to see how much faster they can find their way through an underwater maze if you have nearly drowned them before letting them try, would not have seemed to them to have any bearing on anything they wanted to know. People of this type would like to be able to speak and read languages, but not Anglo-Norman French. They are interested in history, but they have no concentration to read through the vast pamphlet literature of the Civil War in order to make up their minds for themselves about the rights of King and Parliament. They would rather—and so would I, in many periods of history—be guided by those who have been able to give a lifetime to these researches. It is not disgraceful to be dependent on the expert, nor impertinent to be interested in what the expert has to say. Such interests are partly being met today by first-class journalism, by broadcasting and by television, but this is not enough. Lord Robbins has asserted that provision should be made within the universities for this type of student by a great extension of 'general courses'. This calls for debate.

'We have a large number of people of this sort in the universities already, and we have a wastage rate, of students who go down without degrees, of 15 per cent. Dr. Petch's inquiry[1] establishes a general correlation between poor performance at "A" level (i.e. a pass with low marks) and poor performance at degree level (i.e. failure, pass degree or low honours). The wastage rate on present numbers means that each year about 18,000 people go down as failures. I should not wish any boy or girl for whom I had an affection to meet such a failure so early in life. One should, I think, conclude that one in six of those who "qualify" at "A" level have only proved that they can take that kind of examination with that kind of teaching (which one suspects of being devoted Sixth-Form cramming), and that for some this is a peak of achievement, not a springboard for harder studies.

'One-third of graduates are said to get pass or low honours degrees. With a wastage of 15 per cent this means that nearly a half fail to do well. The question must be taken seriously whether people of this type of mind would not get more out of courses which could be developed along the lines that really suit them. Presumably they might get degrees, but this question seems to me of minor importance.'

It is for these people that there is real need to structure courses, not on conventional subject lines, but according to their tastes and interests, following their own approaches to contemporary living and helping them to establish their own connections between various aspects of knowledge. For some an adult version of the project method would be most appropriate. In many respects the better American Liberal Arts College courses provide a similar approach, but it is difficult to get it into acceptable English terms. A most thorny question is where such courses should be pursued. The Robbins Committee turned its back on the idea of separate Liberal Arts Colleges for good reasons, and yet one cannot but fear the heavy hand of the university in shaping such courses. In many ways this general interest in contemporary life and culture is most akin to elements in vocational courses, especially where project methods are envisaged. It may well be, therefore, that we shall need to turn to technical colleges and colleges of education for some experiments in the right type of course for the people that Miss Glover has in mind.

The third category includes all those whose intellectual purpose from the start takes the shape of a vocational interest. It is not for that reason an inferior purpose: we must finally abandon the hurtful and misleading notion that 'vocational' and 'non-vocational' form the inferior and superior tiers of higher education. The vocational shape to an academic purpose has always been a legitimate and worthy one, for there is a fundamental human value in setting out to acquire expertise of a high order for use in human society. But, so the old argument runs, granted that vocational purposes can be quite 'U' in academic courses, the way they are pursued in technical and training colleges is predominantly 'non-U'. Training in techniques is not a liberal education. Whatever substance there may have been in the accusation that this type of course was too much geared to the practical purposes of manipulating things, on the one hand, and knowledge for children, on the other, we must now realize that the very concept of courses both in Technology and Education has been fast broadening out in these last years. What do we mean by the 'educated' technologist and the 'educated' teacher is the question being asked in many colleges. Over the past few years technical colleges of various types and colleges of education have been hard at work shaping and reshaping courses which can genuinely be claimed as higher education. With this experience behind them, they are in a position to command respect for their experiments. The right of freedom to experiment is crucial for them. Here the full meaning of diversification comes out most clearly, for it will be disastrous if, in the attempt to bring the various types of higher education closer together, education courses, for instance, are assimilated too closely to university patterns. On the other hand, a fruitful marriage of technology and education, as suggested in both the following papers, might bear issue in a new type of vocational and humane university. Here we turn to two discussions of the current needs and problems in technical colleges and education colleges respectively.

M. R.

NOTE

1. J. A. Petch, *Before admission performance in J.M.B. examinations compared with subsequent performance at the University of Liverpool* (Liverpool, 1959).

The Technical Colleges
in Higher Education

J. MAITLAND-EDWARDS

The contribution of the Colleges of Advanced Technology in the provision of higher education for the scientist and the technologist is becoming widely known but it is perhaps not so generally appreciated that other technical colleges are far from insignificant in this field. Some Regional Colleges now have larger undergraduate and post-graduate schools than had many of the University Colleges before the last war. A half of the 10,000 students following first-degree courses in technical colleges attend Regional Colleges, although the majority of the 7,000 reading for the Diploma in Technology are in Colleges of Advanced Technology. This discussion will therefore be concerned with technical colleges in general, although for some points the Colleges of Advanced Technology will be considered in particular.

The primary purpose of the technical colleges—and the C.A.T.s have developed from this stock—has always been to provide education directly related to the needs of individuals engaged, or about to be engaged, in industry or commerce, and hence to the needs of industry and commerce themselves. In the present time of rapid technological and sociological change, it is clearly important for the functions of the colleges to be kept under continuous review, but there seems little doubt that their most significant relationship will remain that with industry. This is not to say that the education provided should consist of bare training for specific vocations. The technologist may be described as one who can take initiative in the application of

scientific principles to the operation and evolution of a technology. There is increasing need for such men and women with
sensitivity, thought and imagination, but also with a flair for
discerning the practicable and an awareness of the importance
of human relationships. The technical college student has long
been characterized by his direct personal knowledge of industry
and the current importance of this attribute is evidenced in the
recent phenomenal growth of sandwich courses.

During the inter-war years the technical colleges were populated predominantly by part-time students, the great majority
of whom attended only in the evenings. Part-time day attendance for young people sent to college by their employers increased rapidly in importance during the last war and a very
strong growth has been maintained since, numbers having
trebled since 1947. But the greatest development since the war
has been in full-time (including sandwich) courses, in which the
growth in numbers has been nearly fourfold.

The nomination of the Colleges of Advanced Technology in
1956 to form a spearhead for the development of technological
education has been followed by transfer in emphasis in these ten
colleges from part-time to full-time attendance. In November
1963 they provided for about 12,000 full-time students (including sandwich), some 5,000 part-time day students and
over 5,000 evening-only students. The formation of the
National Council for Technological Awards and the introduction of the Diploma in Technology gave these and the Regional
Colleges a considerable measure of academic freedom to plan
their own courses and to evolve rapidly towards a fuller independence. In 1962 the Colleges of Advanced Technology were
transferred from the financial and administrative control of the
Local Education Authorities, their reconstituted Governing
Bodies maintaining the colleges by means of direct grants from
the Ministry of Education. The relationships at a high level of
these colleges with industry, the universities and the professional bodies have frequently been strengthened by the recon-
stitution of the Governing Bodies, on which the Local Education
Authorities are still represented, but usually in a reduced proportion. The Academic Boards of the colleges which are represented on the Governing Bodies perform functions analogous
to the Senates of some universities, while individual departments of the colleges benefit from the representation of industry,

the universities and professional bodies on their Advisory Committees. Collaboration between the Colleges of Advanced Technology is enhanced through the work of the Committee of Principals. The Regional Advisory Councils, which play a large part in co-ordinating the provision of technical and technological education, establish further valuable links between the various colleges, the universities, industry and professional interests in the regions.

The Colleges of Advanced Technology are planning for a development envisaging a predominantly full-time undergraduate population, with both full-time and part-time post-graduate students. They have proved the worth of courses integrating college instruction with industrial experience (sandwich courses) and this pattern is likely to be firmly retained in the future. It would indeed be deplorable if the unique contribution resulting from the development of these courses were to be lost by the preferential development of simple full-time courses which are admittedly much easier to organize. The plans for the Colleges of Advanced Technology include a diversification based usually on evolving needs, but sometimes arising from experience gained through the introduction of general (liberal) studies into present courses and the potentialities glimpsed in these. Industrial and commercial trends have led to the consideration of trans-discipline courses, e.g. engineering/design; science/modern languages; physics/economics. The presence in the colleges of teachers for general studies, having qualifications and experience in different fields from those previously associated with technical colleges, has contributed to proposals for the development of courses in the social sciences. The colleges are also conscious that they may be in a favourable situation to explore new approaches to the training of teachers, especially for those subjects, such as mathematics, to which a background of technology can bring added realism. Some are already considering their future relationship with University Departments and Training Colleges in this development.

Further extension of research by staff and students is proposed in these colleges and in the Regional Colleges also. Many departments already have a well-established tradition and some an international reputation in this respect. Excellent facilities are being provided. But it is not intended that the primary function, which is teaching, should be obscured by a predominating attachment to research. Indeed, in the context of an educational establishment, the maximum benefit is not derived from research if it is not so organized as to provide enrichment of the quality of teaching as a main purpose.

And it is in the quality of the teaching that many of the colleges could make a valuable contribution to higher education. They are acutely aware that much more needs to be known about the process of learning and the technology of teaching. The value of the tutorial method is now well proven for technology. Project methods have been very widely established in the last five years and are proving a notable advance in securing confidence and independence of thought in students approaching graduation. Currently much attention is being given to exploring the potentialities of such teaching aids as language laboratories, teaching machines and programmed instruction in general. There is little doubt that these will contribute to significant progress when used as adjuncts in a system planned carefully by the individual teacher.

But of critical importance here, as in the whole of Higher Education, will be the ability to recruit staff of high quality to fill the senior teaching, research and administrative posts. The importance of the relationship with industry becomes here again apparent, for if the students need to acquire a 'flair for discerning the practicable and an awareness of the importance of human relationships', they may for many subjects best be taught by those who have developed and proved these abilities in industry. The pattern, already well-established in some countries, of appointments held concurrently in teaching and in industry has much to offer; experiments along these lines have already been made in some C.A.T.s. With the present relatively low age of retirement in various major industrial organizations some retired technologists with the necessary personal attributes, may be able to make valuable contributions.

The vigour which is attending the evolution of the major colleges may itself help to attract teachers of high quality who have a desire to pioneer. The emergency training colleges after the last war were often notable for the vitality and enthusiasm of their students. A similar spirit is not infrequent in the colleges of technology where major changes of administration, organization and public esteem have had repeatedly a tonic effect over recent years. Many may find scope for self-realization in the colleges whose function at the undergraduate level is primarily to provide a balanced education for those who from their school days see their future as being concerned at first-hand with industrial, economic and sociological progress.

The Place of the Training Colleges

MONICA WINGATE

One thing that emerges quite clearly from the Newsom and Robbins Reports is this. Whatever Parliament may ordain neither can be implemented unless the numbers of teachers in this country are vastly increased and their status as a profession raised in proportion.

It may be urged that the second point will take care of itself. If, as is clearly the case, the vital importance of education is beginning to be generally accepted, then the importance of the teacher will need no additional emphasis. Certainly the two things are mutually dependent, since quality of education requires teachers of quality. But this means that we have to achieve them simultaneously, and for this we must create a better public 'image' of the profession as a whole than it enjoys today.

If Robbins offers—as it seems to—the opportunity for lifelong education for every citizen, then excellence and its tangible and mundane rewards must be equally evident in every one of the varied categories of teacher this sort of society will require, whether in primary school, university or college of further education. At present this is far from being the case. Excellence in all types of institution does not gain equal recognition from the general public. We are bedevilled by the assumption that the status of the teacher rises with the intelligence of his pupils. Take only one example. At present, a graduate may teach in any state school including the grammar school without taking the year of postgraduate professional training, i.e. normally after three years as a student. If, however, he elects to spend those three years at a teacher training college he will leave with no more than the right to teach in a state school, and without the degree that most grammar-school posts require. Meanwhile, the degree is becoming, rightly or wrongly, an indispensable symbol of status, in the teaching profession as much as elsewhere, so that promotion to headships in any kind of school is likely to be reserved increasingly for teachers with academic degrees. The tacit assumption behind all this can surely only be that there does not in fact exist for teachers a body of professional know-how, founded upon a serious academic discipline, comparable to that available to other professions, e.g. to the doctor or the minister of religion in training. To teach, therefore, you need to be educated neither more nor less nor differently than those heading for other professions. Specific training or specialized education aimed at your profession is clearly not necessary. In fact to many, including perhaps many of those who themselves are university teachers, such specialized education is a myth and a delusion dangerous only to those who take it seriously. If pressed, some might admit that they thought the real task of the training college was to help those incapable of university disciplines to become better educated at their own level than they are at eighteen, and to learn certain practical techniques under supervision in the classroom, more than this being unnecessary for the teacher of the very young or less able children. Is this a fair description or a caricature? If the latter, barely so! Am I then saying that academic excellence is not important for a teacher? Of course not. What I am saying is that academic excellence is not the only kind and that academic excellence alone, without professional excellence, cannot make a good teacher.

When you look at the reality, the three-year training college, what do you find? After sixteen years I would say: one of the few fields of educational excitement and enrichment remaining in this country, where, within an enlightened Institute of Education, one can still follow experimental syllabuses. Further, the training college shares with the college of technology and of further education that sense of individual purpose and of direction which goes with commitment to a particular goal, but it has the further advantage that the whole body of individual students and staff share the same commitment. Where the different aspects of the curriculum are successfully integrated into a common syllabus, the result is a community with an astonishing unity and vigour, outward-going to the manifold activities of those who live around it. Personal development, through giving and receiving, and a deep understanding of human relationships (that fast vanishing ingredient of the science of living) advance very rapidly in such an atmosphere and community. Is this an idealized picture? Perhaps, but the ideal is surprisingly often achieved.

Turn now to the academic quality of teachers in training. Here there is a considerable overlap with the universities. It is not just that the pitiful potential and attainment of some of those who achieve degrees today would not win them entrance to many training colleges, but, more important, a considerable percentage of training-college students (opinions differ about its exact size) are capable of achieving honours degrees. It is not their incapacity that deters them but the inappropriateness of the goal. As an admittedly rough check on this statement, consider the attainments of those entering training colleges in England and Wales in 1962, as evidenced by their performance at 'A' level in the G.C.E.; 13·5 per cent had gained three or more subjects at this level before entrance. That colleges educating so many young men and women of this academic potential should be regarded as a kind of poor relation of the universities or as leading a lower kind of educational life is frankly ridiculous. But it is also galling and, worst of all, it is dangerous. It is untrue to the facts, but calculated to have a depressing influence upon them until it comes to reflect the actual situation, since it does already deter many of the ablest young men from taking a three-year training and will do so more and more. They need the economic rewards and the prestige of a degree. Early matrimony has helped to keep in the colleges the always high proportion of able young women, since it is widely believed that teaching can more easily be combined with motherhood and matrimony than some other careers. Meanwhile, the older the pupils, the lower the percentage of trained among their teachers. Thus few university teachers have to have a professional training, only one-third of teachers in colleges of technology and further education have had it, and of many grammar school and some degree teachers in secondary modern schools it has not been required. The vast majority, however, of teachers in primary and secondary modern schools have had a training which includes the theory and practice of education. This division in the preparation is exceedingly unhealthy and appears divorced from the real needs of the profession. No country can afford a teaching profession handicapped by such an anomaly, and Great Britain least of any.

What in fact is Robbins proposing to do about all this? First, the Report comes at once to terms with the necessity for opening the degree to the training-college student who is prepared to take four years to get it. This puts him on a level with the four-year-trained university student. How many training-college students are likely to be willing and able to spend four years and take a B.Ed.? The Report hazards the guess that by the 1970's it may be roughly one-quarter of those in the colleges.

At the same time the Report envisages an enormous expansion of the training colleges. They recommend a total of 110,000 by 1973, rising to 130,000 in the second half of the decade. This year, as a result of already very considerable expansion, the colleges contain some 54,000 students only. Upon expansion of this nature most of the recommendations of the Robbins and Newsom Reports will depend. This expansion unfortunately is held to require the continued growth of mammoth institutions. No doubt ways will be found to check the growth within these of suburban isolation and the waning of true community. Modern methods of telecommunication have a big part to play in this, at present relatively unexplored. This is a particularly vital matter for teachers in training who depend in no small measure on belonging to a real community.

The Robbins Report further recommends that schools of education, themselves integral parts of a university, should shoulder the entire responsibility for training colleges and the training of graduates, including their administration, and that their finances should come to them from the Universities Grant Commission. This will sever the close tie of ninety-eight colleges with the local educational authorities, a sad thing for many reasons especially for those of us who work with a good local education authority but rendered inescapable in my view, though the Report does not say so, by the permeation of local government by party politics, from direct contact with which the training of teachers must, as far as possible, be protected in a true democracy.

A most interesting and fertile proposition is that Regional Colleges of Technology should in some cases federate with a training college to 'become in due course parts of universities or universities in their own right'. An advanced course in mathematics or science in such an institution is bound to provide fascinating insights into modern processes and up-to-date equipment far beyond the resources of most training colleges. Students in colleges of technology are often still part of industry and always keenly involved in the industrial and commercial world. They come, for the most part, from the section of the population which Newsom has called 'half our future'. This means that the average teacher will teach in school or further education institutions far more of them than of any other kind of pupil. The staff of these colleges are often empirical and free from academic inhibitions. Moreover the colleges are unique in combining all types of those who teach adults, old and young, from sixteen upwards. There are some who might equally well be doing research in universities instead of where they are, nor will such teachers be engaged only with men and women reading for degrees, but will also include in their pupils some of the less gifted and some who have other goals. Beside them are the teachers of an infinite variety of crafts from engineering to management, while an increasing number of them prepare girls and boys who have deserted grammar school sixth forms for university entrance and scholarly examinations. The colleges themselves are geared to this catholic environment. Much fruitful and some frustrating tension is the result, but it is a tonic much needed by those of us whose field of work cannot reflect as minutely from day to day the needs and values of the community around it. Moreover these have a formidable problem of their own in the fact that rather less than one-third of all teachers in further education have been trained professionally. It is at present a moot question where the training of technical teachers should be done and by whom, but it would obviously be foolish not to make full use of the professional skill and wisdom of the teacher training colleges. For all these reasons and others there is no time to detail, it is a broadening and challenging experience for teachers in training to have some built-in experience of life and work in colleges of technology.

Whatever the advances, and they are very great ones, proposed by the Newsom and Robbins Reports in the field of education, they must be reached through a bottleneck which is the teaching profession. This is a life-size job and it will draw upon all our national resources of finances, man-power, character and intelligence. The better endowed with these any section of the population may be, the greater its responsibility for helping those less well equipped. One warning note must be sounded in a situation full of hope. The worst deficiency in education today is not in the fields of knowledge or technology but in the art of human relationships. Is this the cause or the effect of the increasing emphasis on psychology and sociology? Without these we shall not remedy our deficiency, but something more is needed, perhaps almost too obvious to state. Education is for living but if something called productivity is given priority, then we shall be diverted from the goal. The individual must be set within a group which is willing and small enough to take and use what he has to offer, and he must have something of his own which he is willing to give to the group. Only in this way can he become a person in the Christian sense, for which he needs to see himself as a significant part of a significant whole. The fascinating challenge of the 1960's and 70's is how we are to implement Robbins and Newsom in such a way that the citizens of the future will be better and not worse equipped for human relationships and therefore for living than they are today.

3

Prestige

MARJORIE REEVES

One of the problems we have not yet solved is the relative esteem to be accorded to different institutions and courses in higher education. It is the problem of equality and excellence in an acute form. Perhaps there is no part of the field of education where feelings are so inflamed by intense competition for prestige and by empire-building. 'The whole business of grades and levels and status bedevils higher education at every stage.' In so far as these distinctions are artificially blown up and stand for little except academic snobbery and professional vested interests, they are to be fought and torn down. But the problem is much deeper. People need both success and prestige. 'It is important to give people the experience of success. Too often they are given only the experience of failure or of feeling inferior. Excellence is too narrowly conceived. We don't sufficiently recognize the value of confidence.' 'We all need prestige; we need the respect of others to help sustain our self-respect. We are so constituted as to be sensitive to what other people think of us and to respond to social expectation.' But, granted the fact that we are not all equal in gifts, how best is confidence to be fed and prestige provided in higher education? 'Which is most hurtful, to feel: "I was not clever enough to go to the university and do a degree, I had to go to an inferior college," or to feel: "At the university I was not one of the clever ones, I had to do a despised pass degree." ? ' Whether the argument runs in favour of separating people according to ability or of mixing them, while making an attempt to accord recognition to different sorts and levels of excellence, the basic thing needful is to give a proper status to all. 'It is above all important to try and avoid the conditions which either starve or inflame the need for prestige.'

The Robbins Committee was obviously in a dilemma at this point. On the one hand it tried to set all higher education on the same footing, yet, on the other, it still preserved the division into degree and non-degree courses—although doing a good deal to ensure that the dividing line ran, not between types of institution, only between types of course. It was trying to reconcile two opposed considerations: on the one hand, the desire to preserve something of the traditional degree-structure in this country; on the other, the desire not to impose any sort of a degree strait-jacket on certain types of course. Certainly the diverse kinds of course we have been discussing could not and ought not to be standardized to the conventional degree-pattern: it would be unfair to both sides. Thus, if the degree is held to be a fixed symbol, representing one type and (broadly speaking) one level of excellence alone, there seems no way out of the dilemma. We must, as Robbins suggests, perpetuate a two-tier system of higher education and, since public opinion in this country seems incapable of recognizing excellence except by degree, this means perpetuating in the popular mind an 'inferior' and 'superior' type of education.

The dilemma can, in fact, only be resolved in a way which is educationally satisfactory by adopting a more variable concept of the first degree and being prepared to give it to all who satisfactorily complete a full course of higher education. This would necessitate a clearer concept of what constitutes a 'full course in higher education' than we have at present, and a definite line would have to be drawn between these and other types of *further* education course. In entry qualification (two 'A' levels) and length of course (three years minimum or equivalent) we have already established our criteria and others suggest themselves concerning type of subject-matter and methods. The following, for instance, are examples of the marks which should characterize higher education as distinct from other forms or stages of education (though clearly Sixth Form work already partakes in some measure of this character):

(*a*) The purpose of every course should be to introduce the student to an organized body of theoretical knowledge at a level where he can grasp something of the principles on which that subject is built, its scope, methods and assumptions. The approach may be through a practical or applied interest, but unless the course moves beyond mere practical applications, the student does not achieve that 'freedom of the subject' which is the mark of higher education.

(*b*) Every course should contain some opportunity for work in depth, so that the student has an opportunity of receiving one of the essential experiences of higher education, namely, learning how to master material for oneself: how to acquire, arrange, criticize and interpret a body of knowledge.

(*c*) Higher education should embody a new concept of authority. The student who is beginning to gain the 'freedom of the subject' may listen to authoritative expositions with respect, but yet is entitled to question assumptions and apply techniques of criticism to the very masters from whom he learnt them.

(*d*) Knowledge should no longer be conceived as a fixed body of material to be handed on, but as an ever-expanding territory in which the landscape frequently changes. The assumption should be that teachers as well as students are always learning, and therefore the experience of listening to an expert changing his mind in the light of fresh evidence or thinking fresh thoughts aloud should be another essential experience of higher education.

(*e*) The end to which this intellectual activity is directed is not only the creation of a healthy scepticism and critical acuteness, but also the power to make judgments, to commit oneself experimentally to a viewpoint and to form convictions without closing the mind.

The prestige of the degree would still be exclusive—it would not begin to approach the 'birthright B.A.' caricatured by Dr. Wilson—but it would be shared by a wider range of people than at present. Some courses naturally would not meet present degree requirements and in that sense the degree standard in some cases would be lower. This would be the price to pay for clearing up what is likely to become a running sore in higher education. The Robbins Committee no doubt took soundings of academic opinion and concluded that so radical a departure from recognized academic concepts of the degree would not be acceptable. They were sensible, and yet one remembers that historically the standard of B.A. has often fluctuated with changing conceptions and that a degree should be the servant not the master of good education. If we widened our concept of the first degree now, we could establish a broad basis of common status and prestige which would allay many envies and satisfy many ambitions. On this basic equality the structure of differentiated degrees according to various levels of attainment could be freely erected. Indeed, the fact of such differentiation might be more freely recognized, since once a basic position of prestige is established, acknowledgement of superiority is much more palatable. Is there any real reason to suppose that if a number of 'degree currencies' were operating, the lower would drive out the higher? Would not high intellectual excellence continue to make and maintain its own standard which it would bestow on certain types of degree? For degrees do not really make standards, they only register those standards imparted to them.

Part Four

THE ROLE OF THE SIXTH FORM

Are Sixth Forms really in process of becoming junior colleges of higher education? Quite apart from the controversial question of creating separate colleges for this stage, many of the schools feel that, even as they stand, the life of the Sixth is a kind of ante-room experience to that of higher education. The Crowther Committee, dealing with the age-range fifteen to eighteen, found it could not avoid discussing the impact of universities on the Sixth. The working of the new university admissions procedure has been of vital importance to schoolmasters, while many of them 'waited for Robbins' with the same degree of concern as teachers in higher education. Their attitude towards institutions of higher education is often ambivalent: on the one hand, one of their chief objectives is to obtain admission for their pupils to these places, and therefore they wish to discover 'what they want' in order to gear their teaching to it; on the other hand, many schoolteachers see universities and colleges as corrupting places which corrode the freshness of their pupils and impede good Sixth Form education. The fact is, of course, that the Sixth Form, as conceived in our schools, is both an end in itself and a transition stage from the education of a child to the education of a student. It needs freedom to be itself, but it would be nonsense to deny that one of its most important end-products is young men and women ready to be students of higher education. This is not its only objective, but one of the effects of the Robbins Report must surely be that an ever-increasing proportion of Sixth-Formers almost automatically plan to go on into higher education. Thus the Sixth Form has a crucial role to play as the undercroft on which our whole new structure of higher education must be erected.

The chief question is whether Sixth Form teachers should do their job strictly according to higher education specifications or have freedom to use their own genius in developing this very special kind of education. On the whole conditions in this country have been favourable to the development of an independently-minded Sixth Form staff, of high academic competence, able to hold its own in discussions with university teachers. This tradition has been built up in the past partly because of the deliberate choice by some well-qualified specialists of school rather than university teaching. It would, incidentally, be a lamentable consequence of expansion in higher education if Sixth Form staffs lost their core of academic specialists able to talk on the level with colleagues at the next stage. In joint conversations many attempts have been and are being made to bring into closer relationship university requirements and educational possibilities in Sixth Form curricula, to design 'A' level syllabuses and examinations more flexibly, to give more attention to imponderable factors and less to measurable qualifications. Yet over the last years the constant complaint from the Sixth Form staffs has been of increased pressures ham-stringing their best efforts. Two obvious reasons for this present themselves: first, the mounting competitiveness of entry into higher education which entails forcing boys and girls up to an artificially high standard; secondly, the sheer increase of knowledge, especially in the sciences, which tempts teachers in higher education to demand that boys and girls should be pushed farther along the road before leaving the Sixth Form. It is a large part of the Robbins Committee's intention to reduce the first kind of pressure. If we get anywhere near the desired target of places for all qualifying and desiring, this should ease the kind of situation in which Sixth Formers are set to repeat the same work for another year in order to screw up their 'A' level marks by a few points. Yet, granted the diversification of higher education, there will still be a good deal of differentiation between admissions to varying establishments and courses. Unless public opinion accords a proper esteem to all, Sixth Form work could still be corrupted by the pressures which the superior status of some places exercise. Perhaps when the present extremely competitive situation has abated a little, unhealthy and blown-up emphasis on status-places in higher education will diminish and Sixth Formers will be liberated to do their proper work. Of pressure caused by the sheer increase in knowledge, we can only say that common sense on both sides ought to stop the process of stuffing them so tight that their minds cannot budge. Two distinguished heads of schools write of the kinds of experience which should characterize the Sixth Form years and the difficulties encountered in trying to build these up.

M. R.

158

The Role of the Sixth Form

JOYCE BISHOP

There are so many different ideas of the role the Sixth Form should play today, so many different demands made upon it, that it has to be a kind of chameleon to take on the various colours suggested for it, and I don't think this is very good for it, for it must grow steadily in the colour of its own adoption, the colour which is natural to it as it grows out of certain and sure foundations. I am speaking of the Sixth Form in the girls' schools. In the boys' schools, I am sure it is splendidly different. There it has a longer history—Tom Tulliver went away to boarding-school, Maggie learned what she could from a few lessons or none at home. The boys' schools are surer perhaps in some ways of their aims, for they had their growing pains when the girls' schools still had few problems, at a time when only the really intelligent and academically-minded graced their Sixth Form: I am thinking of the latter part of the last century—and these few in number found no difficulty in entering the women's colleges at Oxford, Cambridge and London. The rest of the school drifted off before they reached this stage, to arrange the flowers at home, prepare for domesticity, in many cases with no hope of wider horizons than those offered by the parental home. For the few there was the hope of matrimony at the mature age of twenty-six or thirty, and for others, uninspiring work in respectable offices, while yet others became ill-paid, over-disciplined nurses or entered on the most soul-destroying, intellectually-stifling training of the pupil teacher.

Girls' education remained a vexed question as it had been since the days of Dr. Johnson—'A man is better pleased when he has a good dinner than when his wife speaks Greek'—and it took another fifty years or more before it occurred to people that the female who spoke Greek might produce the better dinner.

When the first big girls' schools were opened, it took intellectual giants to force open the stronghold of masculine supremacy and these giants rather naturally set tremendous store by the Latin and Greek and Mathematics which was the hall-mark of the educated boy. They introduced an almost monastic discipline so that the chances of matrimony for the educated girl were even less than those for the less intelligent who at least had no inhibitions and suffered only from the fact that female babies survived while the more delicate males—one out of two—expired at birth or very soon after. I expect you know the little rhyme whispered in their own day:

> *Miss Buss and Miss Beale*
> *Cupid's darts do not feel,*
> *Miss Beale and Miss Buss,*
> *How different from us!*

They trained a sort of race of commando troops to assault the gates of the universities and professions, and in my own schooldays at the beginning of this century something of that tradition prevailed. But with the introduction of free secondary education for all in this country, the pattern of girls' education began to change rapidly and now a different world is being met with very different methods. The Sixth Forms are full to overflowing with girls of great diversities of gifts and ambitions: in the Godolphin and Latymer School, for instance—a three-form entry school—the Sixth numbered nearly 200 at the beginning of this term (Michaelmas, 1964), and while this is a great enrichment to the school, we have to be sure that for *all* its members the work and life of the Sixth Form is satisfying and enriching, giving each one a sense of fulfilment. Herein lies our problem and it is one which demands the understanding of the universities and other colleges of higher education.

In the really good Sixth Form perhaps 40 per cent are striving for entry to the university: the others are all hoping for some form of higher education. For nearly all of these the passing of, at least, two subjects at Advanced Level is an essential requirement and this particular hoop is not really the right shape for some of them. They would be far more truly educated if they could pursue a more general kind of curriculum—biting hard into some project or projects which interested them—learning to enjoy the pursuit of a particular bit of knowledge for its own sake, learning something of the correlation and synthesis of knowledge—all of which is denied to those who have to work so hard to master the facts of the Advanced Level syllabuses. They have no time to stand and stare. For the aspirants to the university—and indeed now for some of those who hope to go on to a Teacher Training College—it is not only necessary to pass at Advanced Level, but to gain certain combinations of high grades—and this can and does lead to the pernicious practice of taking the same subjects at successive examinations until the required grades are achieved and yet at the end of all this the candidate is no better educated than she was the first time she took the examination—she has wasted precious months gaining a kind of technical facility for dealing with examination papers. Some can achieve the required grades easily and still have time to be educated, to learn and inquire for themselves, but some have to concentrate so hard on the subjects they are taking at Advanced Level that although the school may provide excellent courses to arouse interest in varied general topics, which these unfortunates are persuaded to attend, they do not drink very deeply or with much enjoyment from these springs of inspiration. Indeed, there is now a real danger, *because* of the demands made upon it by the universities and others, that the examination for the G.C.E., despite all its carefully thought out freedom and flexibility which gave such high hopes to the schools that it could, if used aright, be a valuable measure of discipline and achievement without in any way hampering the really important growth of thought and understanding at the Sixth Form stage, is yet rapidly becoming a kind of Procustean bed which everyone must be made to fit by lopping or stretching—both very bad things for the young. And if to the present demands are to be added those for passes in General Studies and The Use of English, it will become a nightmare as well as an uncomfortable bed.

General Studies—What is meant by these? *What* are they to include? *What* is their real purpose? Some obviously see them as serving much the same function as does the Intelligence Test for the 11 + examination. 'Intelligence' has become the favourite subject of many eleven-year-olds. Will General Studies take the same place in the hearts of the eighteen-year-olds? And what about The Use of English? Can this be learnt in a vacuum? Should not all students learn to use their native language through their reading and their writing on the subjects which interest them? Is their proficiency or lack of it not here for all to see? Do we really want these growing students to think of The Use of English as a subject by itself—apart from the other things they do, and possibly to be thought about no more when the pass is achieved?

The only kind of general studies which are of any use surely are those which grow out of a student's real interests, the pursuit of which will help her to enjoy and understand these special interests more fully because they lead her to some understanding of the synthesis of knowledge. It seems to me tremendously important that in the Sixth Form before the girls go on to the university, they should be helped at any rate to glimpse this, for once there each will become immersed in her own particular specialism which perhaps necessarily narrows as the sum of human knowledge increases. At the Sixth Form stage one way of achieving what I mean is to study the unifying experiences found in human personality rather than to some abstract or general study. For instance, a study of the life and work of Louis Pasteur or Albert Schweitzer or Le Corbusier will reveal how different disciplines and culture meet, for in exploring the relationships between the various aspects of their work, it is possible to find a valid synthesis of a deeply satisfying nature. But these kind of studies need time—an unhurried time—if through them the girl's own ideas are to grow so that she finds something which will be of value to her in all her intellectual work and, indeed, in her approach to life itself.

And so may the universities and other places of higher education never forget—or learn it now, if, as I suspect, some of them have never understood the situation—that in the Sixth Form today we are struggling to ensure that all the members are qualified for the branch of higher education they wish to enter —and this takes some doing as the demands for pre-university specialization increase, I think wrongly, for surely what matters at this stage is the satisfaction which comes to the young student from the mastery of a certain piece of knowledge, the triumph of exactness, the joy which comes of contact with a mind greater—more mature—than her own—or from her own interpretation of a poem, of a picture or a piece of music, by the ex-

acting, but exciting, search for truth in the laboratory or the
mathematics lesson or by the seeing of the ways of God in history or in the beauty and wonder of the world of His creation.
The true value of the girl's work in the Sixth is found in the
kind of person it makes her, and if she is asked to imbibe, retain
and be ready to give out more and more information, to cover
much of the work which used to be done during the first year
at the university, then she may have her passes at Advanced
Level with the required grades, but she will be that much less
of a *person* because she has lacked the time in which to grow,
that much less ready for university work because she has been
stuffed, not allowed to pause and think, with time in which to
develop her own independent judgment.

And in addition to this matter of seeing they get their necessary qualifications and, to my mind, equally, if not more, important, because if we fail here, the girls' last years at school will
be merely stultifying, we are trying to make the Sixth Forms
places of adult judgment, of sound values where their members
can learn to live as equals with other human beings and grow,
not in dependence on a rigid framework, but naturally in a
mature and reasoned atmosphere, in a community which is not
separate from home and the world outside. We should not be
educating them primarily for a particular form of employment,
nor indeed for a particular training, though obviously we must
be constructive and be sure that they are qualified and ready
to proceed with whatever they want to do. But we hear too
much talk of education for this and education for that; it makes
me wish we could keep a clearer view of what education really
is, for I believe that, given the native wit, you can turn a child
into a good scholar, a good craftsman, by instruction and training, but you cannot turn her into anything as fundamental as
a good person. You can prevent quackery and the sacrifice of
reason to fluency and you can encourage disinterestedness and
the rest—so much the most important comes, if at all, as a by-
product, by the Grace of God, for which we can only offer our
most fervent prayers, remembering always the wisdom of St
Thomas à Kempis 'that a humble knowledge of thyself is a
surer way to God than a deep search after learning'. And so, by
making the members of our Sixth Forms aware of their membership of an active, fully functioning community which has
need of them as they of it—and it is this mixture in our Sixth

Forms which makes them such a good thing—we try to encourage the growth of potentialities which will find expression in a satisfactory way of life based upon a living faith. They should learn here to manage relationships as well as to learn useful and interesting things. Many of these Sixth Formers face a real insecurity which former generations were spared, because they meet a wider and much more menacing world and often have less secure foundations on which to stand against the fiery darts of the wicked. It is tremendously important that we have time in which to help these girls to grow up and to get the various manifestations of the conflicts of the spirit into a state of proportion, always resisting the idea of a dichotomy between school and 'the world outside'. This dichotomy did, of course, exist in my day and for many days after, when we lived from the age of about eight to eighteen almost entirely in the ordered world of the school and found its personalities, its politics, its diversions, all absorbing and satisfying. School, to a large extent, dominated our spare time in those unhurried days. There were no coffee bars with their screaming or soporific juke-boxes, no cinemas, very few dances and those in a limited and known circle, carefully scrutinized by parents *very* sure of their responsibilities. Now school, especially the Sixth Form, is not all-sufficient. The steady boy friend is not an unusual phenomenon (and how often the head mistress finds herself sorting out *his* problems as well as hers—does the headmaster help to sort out *hers*?), and clubs and parties, often of a most sophisticated kind, and independent travel are part of the lives of many. Some of them have a social life of which we and, indeed, their parents know little and in this they experiment, sometimes with tragic results. They recognize school as part of a wider whole, not a self-contained world, and see its values soundly and broadly based. They move more freely in that world than we did, and the currency of ideas they gain with us must be valid there as well.

Because of the earlier maturity of the young, early marriage —a certainty now for most girls—and the greater incidence of broken homes, new tongues and manners in the Arts, the immense and far-reaching discoveries of science and the dangers and insecurities of the atomic age, combined here with a new and rather brash prosperity, the increased contact between people of different backgrounds brought about by fast transport and immigration and, more parochially, by the Education Act of 1944, the racial unrest, scepticism and iconoclasm of the age (and the publicity they receive)—because of the complex interplay of all these the school has been forced to widen its horizons, especially for the Sixth Form. This is not a bad thing. It offers even more stimulating opportunity for the education of minds if we in the schools have the elasticity of mind and are knowledgeable enough to take it and are not so pressed by academic demands that we lack the time to see our way through it. Many of our Sixth Formers are honestly trying to find a way to come to terms with life, but their problems are very different and it is not easy to discriminate the immediate needs of the individual at the moment it is often most necessary to do so. We are more often, too, confronted with insoluble and sometimes tragic personal difficulties. We have to make more adjustments in organization to meet the individual case. We *must* regard the Sixth as part of the living organism of society—we have to accept these things as a necessary part of a job, which is, after all, fitting people to live in society and to realize their best selves *and* to advance their frontiers of living a little further towards the achievement of the good life. There is, of course, very real disagreement in our society about the prime importance of the spiritual foundations of these ends and about the means of achieving them. They cannot be achieved by directives, however clear and inspired and authoritative, any more than they could ever be, though these are necessary. They all involve experiments in living and in these experiments of the Sixth Form, we in the schools, whether we like it or not, are involved. We have to be utterly sincere, but never didactic, and never merely conforming in our presentation of principles. It must be in what we are and in what we say and in what we believe, *even when we do not say it*.

These are, I fear, platitudes well known to all of you, but these problems, like the problem of staying human, though specialized, involve an endlessly patient struggle against all the odds from outside, to keep the time-table flexible enough to cater for the individual, and we have to integrate a growing number of out-of-school activities, some of which are not of our begetting, though under our umbrella. What is needed all the time is to provide the means to a synthesis, based on right choice of even more diverse alternatives of action. To be any help in giving them this we ought to have, and have *not*, the mental equipment of a good brains trust, the wisdom of the serpent, the physique of an Olympic athlete. But we can have —we must have—the Sixth Formers' confidence. We must try to know what they are thinking and feeling, what sort of problems they face and we must give them our understanding.

To all this we in the schools are adjusting ourselves by widening the horizons of our own lives, and this is surely good. C. S. Lewis says in, I think, his last book, 'Nothing is ever quite finished with, it may always begin over again. And nothing is quite new; it was always somehow anticipated or prepared for —a seamless, formless continuity in mutability is the mode of our life.' I wonder! Anyway, you in the universities and other places of higher education and we in the schools with our Sixth Forms are still 'Waiting for Robbins'.

2

The Role of the Sixth Form

R. W. YOUNG

As a Scottish head master I am, in company with others north of the Border, attempting to encourage the growth of Sixth Form studies. Most of us are not trying to introduce the English pattern of organization; rather we are groping for the attitudes and ethos which have so markedly characterized the English Sixth Form and which the Crowther Report referred to so admiringly.

The primary role of the Sixth Form is undoubtedly to effect the transition from instruction to study. It is the chrysalis in which the schoolboy or girl prepares to emerge into the outside world and the university as an adult student, responsible for more and more of his own education. This is something which the Sixth Form has by and large succeeded in doing, however vociferous the universities may be about its shortcomings. It was this which made the deepest impression on a Watson's boy who went south some years ago to a L.E.A. grammar school and experienced for the first time the stimulus and interest of Sixth Form studies—a real opportunity to work on his own, to take part in wide-ranging and vigorous discussion and to study in sufficient depth to feel the real challenge of intellectual pursuits. If it safeguards these ideals the Sixth Form will continue to perform its proper function as far ahead as we can see, because in these ways it is justifying its existence not only as a preparation for Higher Education, but as an end in itself—the proper seed-bed for the full development of pupils' abilities and personalities.

The context within which the Sixth Form is currently attempting its job is admittedly not an easy one. Dame Joyce eloquently portrays many of the obstacles which beset us and prevent the Sixth Form from successfully fulfilling its function. In a more general sense I think we are faced with three dilemmas which will not easily be resolved, but whose solution will seriously affect the actual role played by the Sixth Form in the next few years. All these arise from the pressures of the outside world on the schools, and for that reason closely resemble the dilemmas faced by the universities in determining their relationship with Society.

The first may be called the educational dilemma: is the Sixth Form curriculum to be determined in the end by what we believe to be educationally the best thing for our pupils, or by the demands of society, careers, the universities? How high-minded about methodology and content can we be when increased competition for places, together with a much greater emphasis on certain forms of vocational training pull us in a rather different direction. At present, fortunately, the professions themselves do not always pull the same way—to a so-called realistic curriculum, geared, as they say, to the needs of modern society. Scottish accountants, for example, are still insistent on the importance of liberal and intellectual pursuits that bear no apparent relation to the training of an accountant. On the other hand, pleas for the inclusion of Russian, Economics or Mechanics often tend to be based quite explicitly on purely utilitarian and not on educational grounds. I do not myself happen to think that Western civilization depends for its survival on the retention of 'O' level Latin in university requirements. On the other hand I do think that the multiplication of 'useful' skills and examinable know-how is not likely to have educationally good effects on the Sixth Form.[1]

However that may be, we have got to decide, before we find it is too late, whether current social and economic needs determine our Sixth Form education or whether educational considerations come first. We are skilled at compromise in this, I know, but I suspect that in the universities practical realism has already to a great extent won the day; and it may not be possible to hold the balance all that much longer in the schools. Furthermore, the present lack of general education as against specialist training in the universities perhaps imposes on the schools an even greater responsibility to make the right decision here.

A second form of the dilemma is in the field of 'moral education', to use a loose phrase. This was pin-pointed by the recent controversy about premarital intercourse. A foolishly worded editorial paragraph in *The Times Educational Supplement* suggested that since this was now common practice in our society it was unrealistic of schools to uphold an outdated and stricter standard of behaviour. As the headmaster of Charterhouse pointed out, this was tantamount to advocating that the attitudes and standards of behaviour commended by schools should depend, not on our views of what is right or wrong, desirable or undesirable, but on Gallop Poll surveys of the ways in which men and women actually behave in our society at any given time. To put it absurdly, once train robbery becomes common form then it is wrong for schools to deprecate it as an undesirable activity.

There is, of course, a very real problem here. The distinction between convention and morality is not always easily drawn. The temptation to do as the Jones's do is very strong, and the danger of schools becoming cut off from society in their moral attitudes is a real one. The Sixth Form has a vital role to play here. But is this role to follow or to lead? Once again, society does not pull all one way and the schools the other. While recognizing the tension that exists between the outside world of society and the inner world of the school, the outside world itself often urges us to maintain our protected and protective status. Thus the Crowther Report, in pressing for the raising of the school-leaving age, assumes that schools do and should maintain a standard of behaviour far higher than that of the world into which they send their pupils.

A specific form of this same dilemma arises in the field of Christian Education. According to the 1944 Act, the schools were to maintain their essential role as mediators of Christian education even in a largely post-Christian society. How much longer can we continue to do this, particularly in our Sixth Form? The difficulties of doing so are increasingly apparent, I think, to those of us who are Christians. Sixth Form Religious Education is properly based on free discussion and inquiry; but even so the Christian teacher conducts it on the assumption that the school as such is upholding the Christian position. Will society continue to let us do so indefinitely? If not, what will take the place of Christian presuppositions? And what will or should be our reaction? Are we prepared to allow other presuppositions to have the privileged position we enjoy at present? Do we expect to have a situation akin to the universities in which, at best, we can work in neutral territory with the ring being held open, as it were, for all comers? Or shall we be driven back to a much more militant evangelism? In the light of some current radio, TV and newspaper discussions, these questions are not entirely fanciful. Can we assume that the 1944 Act will remain unchanged for ever?

There is yet another dilemma arising from the temper of the times which has already been much referred to: the increasing tension between the outlook of youth and the outlook of older age groups. For schools this means, among other things, that the accepted authoritarian basis of education at school, however skilfully concealed it may be, will not always remain unchallenged. What is to be the reaction of the schools, especially of Christian headmasters and headmistresses—and especially in the Sixth Form?

Each of these dilemmas raises in a different form the question: 'Is the Sixth Form to be the mirror of the society it is designed to educate its pupils for—or not?' If it is, then it must reflect faithfully the needs and demands of society; it must allow itself to be moulded by society, and to fulfil a subservient role, following the lead given by pressures from outside. Or is the role of the Sixth Form rather to be that of a creative minority, itself moulding society by the ideals it lives by, ideals which are determined on grounds independent of society's pressures? Is its role to lead rather than to follow, and, if so, are we convinced enough of our educational ideals, of the attitudes we work to commend, and of the faith we wish to teach, to withstand the pressures from outside? Or rather, perhaps, to tame them, and domesticate them, as it were?

If these questions imply a rather faint-hearted fear for the future, I ought to say that there are many occasions when I feel hopeful and excited about the possibilities of the situation. For one thing, I don't think all the outside pressures are necessarily against us—much of the time society wants the Sixth Form to embody the best intellectual and moral ideals and to go on upholding them. The pressures that point the other way are noisy but perhaps not as powerful as we may sometimes feel. If we speak and act with conviction on behalf of what we really believe in, we may well find more support than we expected— many of our Sixth Formers' parents may appear to be unwilling to stand up for what we believe in for fear of the seemingly ubiquitous Jones, whose children must be kept up with by their children. A convinced and positive lead might well win the support of many of these parents once they knew we and they were acting in concert. In any case I don't see how even an 'autonomous generation' can make up its mind fairly unless we, as Christians, are prepared to make our position as clear as the noisier non-Christians do.

Secondly, I do believe very firmly that the role of the Sixth Form is to provide or be a creative minority in education, and that the situation today is in fact full of possibilities for resolving the three dilemmas I have mentioned. The tension between educational and vocational ideals is capable of resolution, in ways we have not hitherto imagined, through the uniting of theoretical and practical needs, provided we really try to satisfy the whole person during the years spent in the Sixth Form. In morality the modern insistence on realism (much of it admittedly bogus) is perhaps capable of producing attitudes to community and personal rights and duties which might be truer and more satisfying than Utopian ideals on the one hand or cynical realism on the other. In Christian education present-day challenges to the faith may well bring to life a richer and truer apprehension of God than the pietisms of the present and the past. And the apparent divorce between youth and age may well be the birth-pangs of a much more satisfying relationship between the generations than was conceivable within the explicit or implicit authoritarian framework of the past. Indeed if the Sixth Form were to play its part creatively, it might be just the place where solutions to these dilemmas could begin to crystallize.

For the Sixth Form is the crucial meeting-point of intelligent youth and sympathetic age, of idealism and the realism of day-to-day life. I venture to suggest that in the schools we do still have a genuine human contact with pupils of all sorts of levels, so that no special machinery needs to be created to make contacts occur, as appears from the discussions to be the case in the universities. It is no doubt a piece of typical British compromise to say so, but I do feel that if we can be forward-looking without just pandering to the easiest fashions of the moment, Sixth Form education could really be creative in the face of all these tensions. Of course it is difficult to be forward-looking in this way when one is under fire from both sides. But our place as

R. W. Young

Christians is precisely at the point of tension. Nor is there any guarantee that we shall escape the same danger than Alastair McIntyre has pointed out lies in wait for Christian theologians today. Either we cling to traditional ideals so firmly that we lose contact with those to whom we wish to pass them on, because we are no longer understood by them; or we get so much 'with it' that we lose contact with the ideals which we believe our Sixth Forms are designed to embody.

I must sum up—with, I fear, some rather crude generalizations. The primary role of the Sixth Form is to develop as fully as possible the sense of responsibility, the intellectual curiosity, the integrity and the capacities of its pupils, so that from the point when they leave the Sixth Form they have both the power and the desire to continue their education and their growth in these qualities—even if they have to do it on their own. This function, I believe, eclipses all others in importance. It alone would justify resistance to increasing examination demands, to university pressures, to social and economic pleas. It is because the English Sixth Form tradition provides the occasion for that kind of growth that I would like to see a similar tradition established in Scotland.

To fulfil this function the Sixth Form needs, above all, time: time to learn how to waste time (and to know that time is being wasted), time to explore, time to read, time to study in private, time for self-criticism, time for discussion, time to make mistakes and time to learn from them. The danger of most schemes put forward by well-meaning protectors of clear thinking, better writing, more articulate speaking by Sixth Formers—all of these being marks, I suppose, of Sixth Form qualities we want to encourage—is that they reduce the Sixth Former's time and leisure for their own education. And the fallacy of such schemes is that in attempting to legislate against rogues—rogue schools, as much as rogue pupils—they end by merely penalizing the virtuous.

Sixth Form education must be conceived of and organized as an end itself, justifying itself solely by the qualities of mind and character of its pupils. Only then can it also fulfil its other functions as means to some further end. Treat it solely as the tool of society or of the universities and it will not even fulfil that role, let alone the more important one of bringing its pupils to adult maturity and responsibility.

The Role of the Sixth Form

NOTE

1. Incidentally Sixth Form masters (with plenty of help from the universities) are performing one useful function at the moment in relation to overloaded syllabuses. These have fortunately reached explosion point in Physics (and to some extent in Chemistry and Mathematics) so that the Nuffield Foundation (together with Professor Thwaites, the Scottish Education Department and the Ministry of Education) really are cutting some Gordian knots in a determined effort to make more intellectual and practical sense of Science and Mathematics courses. Is it Utopian to hope that the universities will follow suit?

Both the two preceding papers are describing the work of what one might term a crucial 'joint'—a joint in education, between childhood and manhood, between the generations, between the educative community and society generally. This raises once more the question of authority. Perhaps if we were more successful in developing a strong joint here, there would be less likelihood of a break between the generations a little later. Sixth Formers start as (slightly overgrown) children under instruction; they end—many of them—as students ordering their own activities. The new independence and sophistication of young people today makes it easy for them to slip into an apparently self-sufficient way of life of their own, and encouragement is given to this development in many schools by separating the Sixth from the rest in matters of privilege, dress and even sometimes habitation. There is a growing tendency to call these school boys and girls students. Here the schools are rightly adjusting to the new social pattern, but still we ask these Sixth Formers to be learners, to put themselves 'under authority', and in their three-quarter stage between childhood and maturity this is perhaps the hardest thing to ask of them. There is certainly a restlessness amongst many Sixth-Formers. Some simply feel that they will be getting a raw deal in the competition for higher education and therefore develop a grudge against the older generation for betraying them by not thinking sufficiently far ahead. Some gird against compulsory school worship and Religious Instruction and others question the right of the school to uphold any moral standards at all. In so far as they bring a just indictment against the follies of their elders, it must be acknowledged with penitence, but if the Sixth Form is to be a real educational joint we must make it work, not let it break.

What is the 'age of discretion' in choosing whether or no you will attend school prayers and Religious Instruction, play compulsory games, conform to the school moral code and so on? The answer to this question would be debated vigorously, but it is clear that many experienced heads of schools would say that the age of entering the Sixth Form is not the age of discretion, although by the time of leaving they must be ready for, perhaps already making, all such choices. To create a sudden vacuum of authority at any point does not solve the problem; it is more likely to exacerbate it. 'Anti-authoritarianism can be caused among students by the feeling that authority has let them down, that it has abdicated too quickly and is positively leaning over backwards to be liberal.' This suggests that Sixth Formers generally need the support of authority and that the positive affirmations which a school makes in its worship, religious instruction and moral principles should not be withdrawn at this stage. On the other hand, it is crucially important that all such affirmations and assumptions should be freely subject to critical scrutiny and open discussion. Authority must be self-authenticating at this stage or it will be utterly discarded. The important thing is that something should be carried away from the Sixth Form: to be precipitated into the complete open forum of higher education with a vacuum inside can be disastrous. But the difficulties here are critical today. They are discussed briefly by Mr. Gibbs.

M.R.

3

Authority and the Sixth Former

MARK GIBBS

There is restlessness and uncertainty in our Sixth Forms these days, and among those who have to teach them. It has been a fair time cooking—some awkward questions were being asked in London and Middlesex Sixth Form grammar schools long before 1939—but now the temperature is rising perceptibly all over the country; those quiet provincial grammar schools and Scottish academies who pride themselves on their sound learning and traditional discipline are in for some shocks soon.

This restlessness is not to be dismissed as immature naughtiness, or as part of the over-publicized 'teenage revolt'. In essence, it is an entirely commendable desire to question quite ruthlessly many of the educational and ethical assumptions which British grammar schools have had over the years. It may be distinctly uncomfortable to have a young man asking *why*, so much of the time—why do we still have school uniform? Why can't I go to bed with a girl if we both want to? Why do we have to get an entirely farcical knowledge of Latin for X university? Why must I attend school when I have no classes? Why do we have compulsory morning prayers? But if we have been honest, all these years, about wanting to educate people to think for themselves, to be lively citizens and not passive tele-worshippers and pen-pushers, then we cannot complain because they start asking awkward questions.

Nor should we expect them to be content with some of the old authoritarian answers. Very many teachers and parents (and, I fear, particularly Christian teachers and parents) remain very autocratic at heart. We will tend to resent having to give reasons for our traditional discipline and our traditional beliefs. Of course abandoning an autocratic position does not necessarily mean that we abandon all our beliefs or practices (surely, we do have reasons for them?). It does mean that we have to be prepared to defend them, calmly and courteously, and especially when our questioner can claim to be more than just a child. Of course a Sixth Form has to have some disciplined spirit in it, and of course students, like everybody else, often rationalize their selfishness into a facile philosophy of liberty. But this does not mean that we should simply try to impose regulations or standards of behaviour as if eighteen-year-old students have no right to be heard.

In any case, authoritarianism will only provoke cynical amusement in most Sixth Forms these days. We must remember how much half-knowledge of psychology has penetrated far below their ranks: a fourteen-year-old can recognize and despise not merely the sadistic bully (who is rare), but also the emotionally insecure and therefore fussy teacher (a far more common type).

Let us admit, too, that many young adults reckon that we older people have lost any real authority to speak to them, because we have muddled up British education for so long, and because of our own moral confusions. It is not exactly an achievement to have schools without adequate libraries, laboratories or gymnasiums so many years after 1945; and educationalists must share with government officials the heavy blame for the present disgraceful rat-race for university places—after nineteen years' notice that the bulge was with us. (This uncertainty about future courses is itself enough to make any Upper Sixth worried and restless.)

Our nominal standards of personal behaviour and sexual morality may have been clearer, but can we say that in the last twenty years adults in Britain have shown really fine standards of tenderness and consideration in their personal relationships? We have had many years of 'legal' and 'compulsory' divinity teaching and morning assemblies; can we really defend the way we have used these opportunities to put the challenge of the Christian faith before young people? After so many mornings of dull and nominal worship, is it any wonder that many senior students are quietly contemptuous of a Church which seems to offer them nothing but stones for bread?

Nevertheless, I do not believe that many students will exploit an attitude of frankness and openness on the part of their teachers. They know we are not perfect, but they do not expect us to be perfect—the only thing they cannot stand is our pretending always to know best. If we can give our Sixth Formers the compliment of treating them as young adults—and even of arguing with them as adults rather than condescending to them as children—I believe this can be a great strength in our educational system in the strenuous days ahead. We and our students must be in some sense partners as we take the strain together.

reaction. The students of his teacher showed up this impressed
upon the patients, which by then they had advanced mostly in year
until he came to their beds. However great or so indifferent of
the surgeon who performed the operation, and to his parent of
a somewhat less sanguinary
and affliction to consider the disease you may...

Part Five

THE SPRINGS
OF INTELLECTUAL VITALITY

The role of the highly-educated is increasingly important in society, the 'vocational' aspect now implicit in most courses in universities and colleges is a true and honest one—but can we base our whole expanding enterprise of higher education, with the further research which attaches to it for some, on these practical values alone? Is there not in the background of all our immediate problems a much more fundamental question: *What keeps human beings intellectually alive?* 'Man does not live by bread alone . . .': one might say 'Man's mind does not live by utility alone,' but then, how does one finish the statement? What *does* it live by? One has the feeling that unless we discover the answer to this question all our planning will be of no avail. We shall only be creating, or extending, dreary morasses of learning through which students blunder, even if they do not stick fast, with never a life-giving spring or fast-flowing stream to refresh them.

Of course this is an extreme picture. Some people do come to college with the springs already flowing; many who begin with a utilitarian intent find intellectual excitement welling up in their minds. But we have already drawn attention to a widespread academic *malaise* among students today which is attested by many teachers, and our present preoccupation with making more and more room for students takes no account of this intellectual crisis. At various points in this book we have discussed some of the more general causes of student unhappiness, but we must now ask more specifically: why does their intellectual curiosity fail? Why do so many never achieve any real degree of integration with their studies? It is significant that the mood of academic disillusionment often comes on them in their second year. This suggests that the limited motive of getting a place in higher education has carried them over the threshold and a certain way along the road beyond before it peters out. But it also suggests that unless a more fundamental and long-term motive for study can be established, if possible while still at school, these boys and girls will not have enough momentum

183

to carry them through college at any kind of creative level. Is it a sad but inevitable fact that schools have no time to light up and foster intellectual curiosity because they are so busy procuring for pupils the right status-symbols in education? Dame Joyce and Mr. Young would fight for the principle that 'knowledge for its own sake' is certainly the business of the schools, and we would contend that unless we all make it our business, universities and colleges are lost.

This is, of course, the old liberal ideal and we have to ask whether it is any longer tenable. Were there not thirty, forty, fifty years ago stable conditions—or the remnants of stable conditions—which gave the necessary foundation conviction that culture and learning would go on? History was worth studying because history would go on. Have not these circumstances now given place to conditions which are really inimical to the fostering of intellectual enthusiasms and the capacity to become wholly absorbed in some area of knowledge remote from practical considerations? The insecurity of world peace and the burden of world needs—brought so much nearer by mass-media—often lay on the young such urgent pressure to action that 'knowledge for its own sake' appears to them as a form of selfish indulgence. This, at any rate, is how many of them argue. Furthermore, as we have already said, there is a strong urge towards doing things together among the young today: this favours practical forms of training and activity and perhaps even puts laboratory work in a more attractive light than library work. The more theoretical one's studies become, the more they must be wrestled with alone in the mind, demanding a price in terms of austere withdrawal which is hard to pay today. Finally, may it not be said that all the quick ways in which curiosity can be titillated and easily satisfied—radio and television talks, articles in Sunday papers, books with more pictures than text, reviews which can be a substitute for the works themselves—are fast unfitting us for the studious activity of sitting down for two or three hours at a stretch to read big books that demand close attention? The word 'us' is used advisedly, since some, if not all, the conditions suggested above are undoubtedly affecting the life of dons as well as students. Do any of us (that is, any in the appropriate age-bracket) find long-term intellectual pursuits as easy to place in the centre of our lives today as, say, thirty years ago?

184

But why should we? Does long-ranging and deep-going thought and study really matter to the masses in higher education, either of teachers or students? Is not this kind of activity the esoteric preoccupation of the few on whose intellectual vitality all the rest can live? This is not a question that is answered by argument so much as by conviction. One thing is clear, however, that if we do hold to the conviction that the most creative part of intellectual experience for both dons and students is the lighting up of the mind by the pursuit of some piece of truth for its own sake, then we must find ways of justifying—still more of communicating—this conviction to a generation that does not regard it as axiomatic and is often cynical about all academic motives. In the following paper Professor Butterfield discusses the whole question of intellectual vitality in the context of academic institutions and teaching.

M. R.

The Springs of Intellectual Vitality

HERBERT BUTTERFIELD

Sometimes, when one is invited to speak at a conference, one brings only the half-attention of a distracted mind to the question of the subject which one is being asked to discuss. The title, 'The Springs of Intellectual Vitality', is certainly calculated to catch the eye, and produces, I suppose, some romantic vibrations—it is a seductive title for a lecture to which one is committing oneself many months ahead of the appointed date. I must confess myself to have been very absent-minded, and, when the sobering moment finally came upon me, I recollected how, for some time, I had been brooding about my own lack of the very thing I was being asked to talk about. During the only vacant moment of my day—the time when I shave—I had recently been asking myself where on earth this intellectual vitality took its rise. In those grey and gloomy dawns that we were having in July and August, I wondered whether perhaps everything did not depend on the pace and pressure of the blood running through the brain. I wished that I had offered to write a paper on the drying-up of inspiration and the lack of intellectual vitality; for, though I doubt whether I could have thrown much light on even that, I think I could have described the experience.

The appalling range of the topic is fortunately limited when one is raising the issue in a programme of discussion which is concerned with higher education. And there is a comparatively easy way of breaking into the subject if one begins by inverting it; for everybody is aware of the things which damp down vitality and reduce teaching establishments to mere routine. For one thing, though examinations, besides being necessary, can even be useful instruments of education (and though I have no reason for objecting to them personally, since I always felt that I came off better in them than I ought to do), they are tending to become more important and in various ways more dangerous than they used to be. Students, parents, administrators and politicians, instead of seeing universities as places where minds are trained and young people are educated, come easily to thinking of them as machines for putting masses of students through examinations. The emphasis is changing, partly owing to alterations in society itself, partly owing to the character of some new subjects, and partly owing to the growing influence of a public opinion only partially aware of the issues involved. It is perhaps inevitable that, in a technological world, the examination, the purely technical qualification, should become more important than ever before, the university degree coming to be regarded as more like the test for entry into a profession. Possibly we are developing a kind of world which can only be run by professors, Ph.D. students and good examinees; and this itself could be a grave misfortune, even apart from the fact that it might leave the really brilliant people—the ones who ought to be governing us—with nothing to do except to organize fascinating mail-train robberies. If examinations are going to have a key place in our society, we ought to reflect on the way in which the culture and life of China seem to have been stultified by the dominance of an official examination-system.

Even in examinations it was always necessary to be on guard against a tendency to think that the accurate reproduction of curriculum knowledge (the submission of the expected answer) was the important thing. There have been times when originality itself has been penalized by examiners too anxious to receive from the candidates the expected answer, too anxious just to see whether any requirement has been omitted. The outside world is always liable to be too mechanical in its ideas on this subject, and this can be dangerous, because it leads almost inevitably to an unfortunate development. A world that feels an urgent need for great numbers of people simply qualified up to a certain level in a given technique, soon tends to think in terms of mass-production and to look for short-cut methods. It comes to expect that universities will set out to provide just the most economical way of achieving examination results. Examination methods are themselves liable to be defective, and in certain fields they become less satisfactory as the number of candidates becomes greater. Harder forms of criteria come to prevail; greater importance comes to be attached to mere memory-work. It is possible to provide students with a dessicated kind of history, reduced to note-form, suitable for memorizing, and adapted to purposes of sheer recapitulation. The teacher may attempt to predict the questions that the examination-paper will contain—offering eight topics of which some four are guaranteed to appear in the next paper. Even the natural sciences may be taught too directly for examination purposes, which means an evasion of the reference to fundamentals, an attempt to cover a curriculum without sufficient attention to the training in thinking. When scientists want to exclude from their examination those exercises in continuous English to which their predecessors attached importance, one wonders whether the care for the curriculum is not being allowed to supersede the educational objective—whether there is not an excessive concentration on mere technique. It would be well if, besides examining competence in a given curriculum-subject, we could find ways of testing the good which the study of the subject has done to the student's mind. The greatest of all the virtues of education may depend on the imponderable things that are super-added, the things that come over and above the formal syllabus.

If the university is to be a place of intellectual stimulus, it is clear that teachers must not be regarded as mere reproducers of knowledge, separated too radically from the researchers, who are supposed to be creative. Those who in recent years have called for a radical division between teachers and research-workers, have asserted sometimes that the former must have the same prestige as the latter. But the whole intellectual context of this assertion—the mere fact that such a thing needs to be said—is sufficient to show that, on this system, the status of the teacher would be reduced. (Prestige does not come at a word of command in the way that is sometimes taken for granted.) In America, where this radical separation sometimes exists, it seems to have the effect of making the subject of study harden more quickly into routine. It comes to be conceived as a teaching subject, in which everything is 'taped' and everybody soon finds himself locked in a conventionalized curriculum. Where there is some degree of contact with research it seems possible for the teacher to communicate knowledge in a more fluid state; and, then, for the student, this knowledge becomes a field in which the mind can have some play. The student is given a notion of the way in which knowledge is manufactured and he pierces through the conventional screen, breaks through to things that are fundamental.

Intellectual awakening seems to come to young people in a variety of ways. It can be produced by the reading of a book. I met the case of a boy who saw no point in literature and resisted all attempts to turn him into a reader, until, just before his middle 'teens, the essays of Max Beerbohm lit in him a fire that never seemed to go out. Those of us who belong to the teaching world must have observed how very important the influence of the home environment must be in this connection. Because, nowadays, there are so many young people who do not enjoy this advantage within their own families, the present topic has become a more urgent one for schools and universities. One notices sometimes that the appointment of a new teacher in a college can quickly bring about an amazing change in the intellectual quality of the students who are working in his field. If one asks whether the success is due to the man's skill in the selection of scholarship candidates or is the result, rather, of dynamic teaching, one discovers, I think, that mere discernment in the award of scholarships is not very effective unless something in the character of the teaching itself gives drive to the student after he has come to the university.

It would seem that there are successive stages at which a student needs almost to be 'born again'. An awakening can take place in the later years at school, and, at this stage, a tremendous interest can be aroused in a given subject. There is a sense, however, in which a new revolution ought to occur at the university, where students often expect to carry on in the way they have done at school. They regard themselves as preparing for an examination; they think that what they need is a lot of 'spoon-feeding'; they are anxious to know what is the expected answer, or what will please their teacher; and they tend to think in terms of getting round the examination requirements. The result is that even the young people who are promising need almost to be coaxed into a certain degree of intellectual independence, or driven to seek sincerity at a deeper level than before. Yet, once they have discovered themselves in this way, and have come to realize their larger liberty, this itself seems to give them a certain exhilaration. In some subjects (and this would include my own, I think) it might be good policy, if one wished to give a student a great drive, to encourage him primarily in the field where he has special interests and aptitudes; since, once he has gathered momentum, he will more easily catch the other things into his sweep. If one were too intent on the examination requirements and tried rather to bully the man where he was weak, the result, in all probability, would be less happy. Since the stimulus is the important thing, it is excellent, at least in a subject like history, if the passage from school to university entails a considerable change of syllabus. Those who have been modernists in their later years at school can experience quite an awakening if they are compelled suddenly to confront the strangeness of the medieval world, which calls for different exercises of the imagination and requires so many transpositions in the mind. When good people have been too wearied by preparation for scholarship examinations, it has been necessary on occasion to take them away from history altogether for a time, and freshen them up with work perhaps of a more literary nature. But the greatest danger is just to continue working in the way one worked at school; for students at the university like to rely on what they did at school. Yet here it is most difficult to persuade them to pierce to the fundamentals—to break down a framework of knowledge that has become too firmly imprinted on their minds and memories. Here is the point where they most resolutely refuse to be 'born again'. Even with young university students, one ought in fact to play dizzily at times on the frontiers of knowledge, since this is so capable of producing a quickening and a feeling of exhilaration. It is the introduction of schoolma'am methods in the university to meet the needs of examinations which is the most deadening thing of all. On the whole, however, if one attaches importance to being 'born again' at the university, this process calls for such different treatment in different cases that some form or some degree of individual teaching is a momentous thing if it is possible at all.

One cannot avoid the feeling that the original work which is done at the very top level in universities—whatever the ultimate forces behind it—has something to do with the intellectual exhilaration that exists amongst the juniors; so that it is wrong ever to consider universities as merely teaching institutions.

The Springs of Intellectual Vitality

Within a given university a certain school of study or a certain laboratory may be particularly distinguished for its intellectual liveliness and its stimulating atmosphere. This can happen when, in the upper reaches of a department, men are advancing into exciting realms of discovery, but, at the same time, the interest of all this is not too local or refined—not too far removed from the ordinary teaching work. A tremendous intellectual liveliness (which I felt to be like a 'renaissance') seemed to occur in Cambridge amongst quite a nest of scientists a few decades ago. They seemed to give stimulus to everything around them, and much of this appeared to spring from their interest, not merely in special discoveries, but in the general implications of science, and its relations with everything else. I never quite knew how much this may have owed to a single individual; and I think that certain aspects of Marxism may have helped to provide the stimulus. Here, what is important is the excitement in the atmosphere, or the mood of exhilaration, which infects everybody who comes near, catches them into itself and sometime stimulates the young to something more than they had thought themselves capable of. If one looks at the list of people in the Cavendish Laboratory in about the year 1925—looks at the young as well as the old, and bears in mind what happened to the younger ones in later years—one can hardly escape the impression of the intellectual stir that must have been taking place there: so many people in such a state of expectancy and all knocking sparks off one another. This is the picture that the world ought to have in mind when it thinks of universities—to offset the notion of them as glorified high schools, existing to get students through examinations. If one thinks of the social life and the general experience of undergraduates, one might feel that the ideal size for a university would be a body of about 2,000 students. But, apart from the need to cater for the specialized branches of a subject, a department needs a larger staff than this would allow—needs bunches of people who provide a lively intellectual exchange and keep one another on their toes. From this point of view 3,000 students would probably be the very minimum for a university.

So far as one can gather from people who have been engaged in the arts—in music or poetry or the novel for example—the atmosphere of Cambridge provides little encouragement for genuine creative work on the imaginative side. The intellectual climate in Oxford may be rather different; but we in Cambridge do appear to have shortcomings on this side. Of late we have been inclined to pride ourselves on the fact that, for a short time between the two wars, we had in our midst the Festival Theatre, which was bold enough to try experiments. But, while it was with us, I am not sure that we supported it well; and, if High Table conversations could kill, its life would have been shorter than it really was. When young people tell me about plans of theirs that touch the Fine Arts or say that they are trying to establish a literary magazine, I encourage them as much as I can, but I tell them to fortify their inner souls, for Cambridge will crab anything they attempt. I tell them that, if, in spite of the crabbing they will carry on for a while, then, once the enterprise has finally been wound up, it will be praised to the skies, and there will be no end of people to express their regret. And if, after that, they survive beyond the age of eighty, they will be greatly honoured—honoured even perhaps beyond their deserts. It is possible that, in the academic world, the critical faculty is too sharp, and each man is a little afraid of the destructive power of all the others. At the same time, the people who write poetry and novels seem to have a more serious criticism to make; for they feel that there is something constricting in the atmosphere of Cambridge which throttles the creative instinct in them. I, who used to think that if you found an empty room at the top of a house, you could escape from surrounding circumstances and soar to infinity, must now accept what I am told, and believe that the poet had better go to the moors and the novelist retreat to a Mediterranean island. The academic mind is chiefly defective on the imaginative side, and the academic world not always sufficiently appreciative of imagination. I have known people who have avowed that they would not tolerate such a thing in students of history. If the Fine Arts had a higher place in education, there might be more creative work even in the university world.

Yet perhaps there never was a time when, in so many fields, the intellectual leadership passed to the universities, to the degree that it has done in the mid-twentieth century. The result may not be entirely happy if the professional mentality acquires too great an ascendancy on all sides; and we may wonder if it is not the spread of an academic kind of literal-mindedness which submerges the business of the state (or the business of the university) under tons of roneoed paper, some of which preserves the record of things which surely it would be more business-like to forget. The roneoed paper seems calculated to oppress the imagination and check originality. And here is another reason why we may end by landing ourselves in a bog—going the way that China went in former times.

It seems that there are defects in all teaching establishments, partly because the number who teach must be greater than those who are born teachers, and partly because of the tendency to drift into routine. It seems to be an enormously difficult thing to alter the curriculum in a university that is long-established, so that the new university has become doubly important as providing at least a field for possible experiment. The development of a subject may be constricted by the very nature of the university institutions in which the subject is being pursued. When one considers from what miscellaneous realms the scientist has occasionally caught a hypothesis (sometimes from influences in the world of humanism or from branches of science not really his own)—when one remembers the kinds of cross-fertilization that can occur between differing subjects, or the important work now being done in those borderlands where the various branches of either science or the humanities meet and overlap—it becomes difficult to resist the view that the high frontiers between university departments must sometimes have been a check upon free development. In any case there are important periods of history in which the exciting intellectual developments have taken place outside the universities. And it almost seems as if, in the universities, there is a tendency to envisage the future as only a case of going further and further in the direction in which one is now moving—a trend simply to greater elaboration and a minuter subdivision of knowledge— all of which means that subjects tend to develop into 'scholastic' systems, that make it harder to change direction or to go back to basic principles and make a new start. Because of the germinal things that so often arise outside the academic world, it is important that universities should keep their windows open, keep themselves accessible to every breeze that comes from out of doors—taking note of the new things that emerge from the needs and demands of society in general. The effective genesis of that fairly rarefied product which I call 'academic history', and which came to maturity in Ranke, took place in the University of Göttingen in the later decades of the eighteenth century, when that university had its windows open to the outside world and was trying to give a training in statesmanship to young aristocrats who were destined for public service.

While this is the case, it may still be true that the danger to universities today comes from the opposite side. The prestige of the university tradition has caught the eyes of governments, parties, industrialists and democratic peoples, who may want to reduce the system to serve too directly their own purposes. An easy surrender to such a policy might end in the destruction of that very prestige which had made the system originally so desirable. We ought to note, therefore, that the historians at Göttingen, though they opened their minds to the outside world, seem to have taken care not to lose command of the situation. They developed that fairly austere thing which we call 'academic history', and they could not have done this by any mere surrender to current fashion. In fact, we can see them picking and choosing from the multitude of things that the outside world had to offer them—adopting some of the ideas of the French *philosophe* movement, but rejecting others that were very fashionable—adopting also ideas from what we today would call the Romantic movement. Here were two germinal non-university developments in the intellectual life of the West, and these men captured stimulating things out of them, while keeping their academic criteria in mind. The total result of all this was a new synthesis. If we today were to say that universities should set out to reflect just the ideas of contemporary society, so that they become merely the mirrors of intellectual fashion outside their walls, we should fall into the kind of materialism which is always calculated to quench intellectual vitality. One can admit that there are serious defects in the academic mentality without blinding oneself to the constrictions and distortions that are produced by forces and factors, still more disturbing, in the outside world. It is better to work for the opening of archives to the free play of scholarship than to be at the mercy of bands of official historians, who are admitted to the documents but are not always proof against the fallacies that arise out of their own position. It is better to see the sciences developing out of problems as they arise in the laboratory than to have scientific study going lop-sided because everything has to be subordinated to the needs of a possible war. There are universities in the world which are evidence of the fact that the policy of surrendering to outside forces can easily end in mere submission to political domination. One of the necessary conditions for intellectual vitality and for that kind of exhilaration which leads to really creative work, is the existence of universities in which people can feel that they are pursuing knowledge for its own sake, going forward with their inquiries, even if the results may be inconvenient for the time being, or their utility is not immediate. The greatest consequences seem often to come from discoveries the utility of which was at any rate unpredictable. The universities must in any case assert the importance of free discussion, and insist on the enormous value of sheer intellectual exchange, unhampered by political or ecclesiastical orthodoxies. If thought is limited externally at any point—if the historian works in the knowledge that a certain area of his field or a certain line of thought is taboo—the limitation almost inevitably affects a larger area of the field than that which is ostensibly under prohibition. In fact, 'restriction' itself may be less important than the further intellectual 'constriction' which it almost automatically produces. And the mere fact of having to be on one's guard is just the thing that may prevent the mind from taking to the air. A vice-chancellor from a country not now in the British Commonwealth—and one who claimed that he had been no particular friend of British supremacy—recently put to a conference the question: 'What universities were ever more like ivory towers than Oxford and Cambridge in the nineteenth century?' He then caused some sensation by adding the question: 'And what universities ever trained better Civil Servants?' Nobody would suggest that a university in these days should be like an ivory tower, but, if on the one hand we can say that it is good to open the windows to the world outside, it may be useful to remember also that there sometimes has to be retreat and withdrawal before anything really creative is achieved.

For all these reasons, universities need, and ought to prize, a certain kind of autonomy, and, in particular, autonomy in the intellectual realm. It might be said that, in the last resort, there is an element of paradox in this autonomy, since, in these days at least, it virtually has to be conceded by the state. Let us say that for the sake of society and for the sake of the future, the state would be wise to grant and guard this autonomy. And we ourselves ought to play up 'the idea of the university' for the very reason that so many people play it down—it is a source of both the prestige and the intellectual exhilaration that our system enjoys. Universities, in other words, ought on the one hand to be regarded as international (or at any rate non-national) institutions; and on the other hand ought to be accepted as designed to promote scholarship, education and intellectual exchange rather than to assist other more immediate, more utilitarian objects of society and government.

I have said nothing about the idea of a Christian university, or the notion that, in any intellectual society, a basic unity of outlook is apt to produce a galvanizing effect. One might have expected (and all of us, no doubt, would have liked to say) that the laying hold on a spiritual religion, besides altering men's outlook, is calculated to give a tremendous impulse to the intellect. Whatever truth there may be in this is liable to be more than cancelled, however, firstly, if one is born into a hereditary religion that has become conventionalized, and secondly, when the spiritual order of things has become too inextricably entangled with mundane systems.

The question of the relations between the Christian religion and the whole problem of intellectual vitality is not an easy one, especially in view of a danger which must, I suppose, affect all forms of religion. The danger lies in the tendency to stress the fact that the truth has been revealed, the essential things are already known; all of which may be correct in a sense, but becomes unfortunate when the truth is encased in a few hard formulas, as though here were the end rather than the beginning of questing—a closing-in of thought instead of the opening-out of a mystery. Perhaps the greatest jolt that the Christian student of history ever suffers is the discovery that our faith, not only in its entanglements with mundane systems but even also in the religious developments, so far as these are externalized and visible to the historian, is subject to the same laws and processes as other religions—as the ancient Hebrew or the medieval Islamic, for example—it is not guarded from these dangers by any special Providence. It was probably this which led Lord Acton to say what may be the most shocking thing ever said about history by a Christian—namely, that he could see Providence in general history, in the secular history of mankind, but that there was no Providence in the history of the Church. The remark is perhaps an understandable one; but it is one of a number of things which show that Acton did not take sufficient account of the life that has a purely spiritual reference.

There are times when the domination of a recently-victorious religion seems to be accompanied by great intellectual exhilaration in the people who are conscious of being the winning party. This may have been true at various times in the history of Christianity; but it seems to be true also of Marxism—it is a thing that may be true irrespective of the actual content of the faith that has come to the top of the world. But Christianity became entangled with mundane régimes, monarchical, aristocratic, theocratic, etc., and also with mundane intellectual systems—men came to imagine that it must stand or fall with the Aristotelian cosmology, for example. Because they defended these systems as things which were essential to the cause of religion itself, the Churches in time became the chief agencies of repression, even the enemies of scientific discovery. It is because of this that, throughout some of the centuries of modern history, they present the unfortunate spectacle of almost continuous intellectual retreat, as a result of which their thought, even today, may be too much drawn in, too much on the defensive. We today would say that the retreats were unnecessary; or, rather, the Churches ought never to have been in the position of regarding them as retreats; especially as the successive attacks in recent centuries have merely compelled Christianity to be more spiritual—have forced it to confide in the purely spiritual—a state of things which ought to have existed all the time. But the incidental losses, the mundane losses, resulting from this posture and this policy have been very great in recent centuries. I always think that a lot of such truth as is comprised in Marxist history ought to have been brought out first by Christians; and it would have been better—more unmixed with harm—if it had been proclaimed to the world initially by Christians. But the Christian intellect was otherwise occupied, defending, in the mundane sphere, what were so often the wrong things. There are certain mixtures of religion and mundane systems which are capable of being more sinister than worldly-mindedness itself, because they may have the effect of introducing religious sanctions to double the force of existing evils. Religion ought not even to be so mundane as to make intellectual vitality its actual objective. But if one could disentangle the spiritual from time and place, and extricate it in these days even from the inheritance of Greece and Rome, it is possible that the process would have by-products which intellectually would be generative.

One of the questions which I should like to be able to answer, but which my professional colleagues sometimes think it is wrong to ask, is the question why, since the opening of the Christian era, it is Western civilization that has proved intellectually so dynamic. When I think of a particular example or occasion, like the Renaissance, I am prepared to attribute a good deal to the stimulating economic life; also I can see why something like a city-state should be more intellectually stimulating than any other kind of city. At the same time I can understand how a long-standing religion can be a factor both constricting and depressing—I think Islam may have checked the development of that Arab culture which for a considerable time under the same religion had moved quicker and further than its Christian counterpart. Established forms of Christianity can have the same deadening effect, and possibly did so in the case of Orthodoxy in Russia and Catholicism in Spain during recent centuries. I regret that anything should have provoked the Reformation, and I would say that I regretted the Reformation, except that I suppose I really mean I regret there having been any necessity for it. But I have a feeling that, if the Reformation had failed, the world, though ultimately settling down into a comfortable acceptance of an orthodoxy and an authoritarian system (and though much more free from turmoil and conflict than in reality it proved to be) might have relapsed into the rigidity of the great oriental civilizations.

Yet the Church played a great part in the beginnings of education in our quarter of the globe, for it saw that even primitive peoples must have the Bible. To the Church we owe also the development of our universities, which from the first were supra-national institutions. And under the presidency of our religion our culture developed, Christianity affecting it throughout its formative period, and the profounder results of this remaining with us even after the religion has been secularized out of it. If people tell me that economic individualism is the ultimate source of the galvanic character of Western culture, I cannot help doubting this notion of a single cause possessing finality, nor can I help asking myself what lies behind economic individualism itself. There is one big factor to bear in mind when we are considering the dynamic individualism of Western culture. Our peculiar type of freedom emerges from a belief about the nature of man himself—each human being an eternal soul with a value and a validity extending beyond all time—incommensurate therefore with anything else in the visible universe. Each human being has an eternal dimension that the state itself cannot have, because, as Acton said, society does not possess an eternal soul. Here and in other respects, certain fundamental assumptions concerning man himself, and concerning the whole human drama, sprang out of religion, and had a chemical influence in society—operating sometimes against ecclesiastical authority itself, operating now through dissenters, now even through lapsed Christians. There is in the Christian view of education the idea that the object is the saving and the making of the individual man—his enrichment, and the eliciting of his potentialities, and the preparation for the good life or for what is sometimes called fullness of life. In our modern secularized world, it means putting a man in a position to judge fairly for himself the God whom he will serve or the intellectual system he will adopt. He is not to be regarded as a unit just to be drilled into a social scheme which harnesses everybody for the sheer purpose of conquering and exploiting the physical universe. And, as this latter enterprise, if carried on unmitigated, will lead men to greater covetousness and war— and, even short of that, will depress the finer functionings of the intellect—it is possible that the Christians, by their concern for all the more imponderable things in man and in life, have a special part to play in the discussion of the university problem at the present time.

The drive for knowledge as useful power is an important source of immediate intellectual vitality, but power is a rank-growing plant that can crowd out others. When human beings reach the point where the only question they can ask is, Of what use will it be to me? they are creating for themselves an intellectual and spiritual desert where nothing grows except the instruments of their power. Awareness of shape, colour, texture, sound, response to the creations of men's minds and imaginations, delight in things and persons for their own sake, these have all died. They have died because, at the centre, conviction about the meaning of human experience has died, smothered by this all-powerful desire to choke the independent life out of everything and reduce it to the status of a tool.

In a subtle sense the drive for mastery can kill awareness and sensitivity right in the heart of the intellectual activity itself. We all know the immense exhilaration of mastering an intellectual problem: 'Now I have really got that completely taped and under my hand! I *know* it!' The techniques by which we master—dissecting and analysing, categorizing and organizing —are the techniques of power. It is easy to get so drunk with intellectual power in this way as to end by claiming that in mastering we have taken full possession, so that there is nothing left unknown, no mystery, no surprise, no wonder. But this is the death of delight which is a response to something recognized but not possessed and infinitely more knowable. It can also be the death of true intellectual curiosity, since fresh knowledge tends to be sought, not for its own intrinsic excitement, but to gain further experience of mastery.

Can we save delight from being murdered by this craving for power? Dr. Jenkins raises this question:

'Can we afford to assume that delight in a subject will always be present and self-generating, when by delight we mean, not only aesthetic satisfaction but something which comes from seeing meaning in what one is doing, although it has no immediate utility, in relation to other parts of one's experience?

This depends on a more general apprehension of meaning in life, and education is now conducted in a situation where many people do not see meaning and, finding this intolerable, tend to become destructive. I knew someone who was convinced by Wittgenstein that there was no point in philosophy and was honest enough to give up. Luckily he had other resources, including a stable social situation and so was able to make another life. No people or society has lived long without conviction. Even if we manage a stable society in which education can proceed, there will be a gradual attrition of delight in one's subject, because of a lack of meaning in the whole. The result will be triviality and pedantry and a moving away from those subjects which are delightful to study into the fields of utility and into administration with all its dreary apparatus of power.'

Both Professor Butterfield and Dr. Jenkins are surely pushing the question back to that of the nature and destiny of Man. There will naturally be sharp conflicts of belief on this, but would there not be much agreement with the contention that real activity of mind and spirit is deeply connected with belief in the significance of individual human beings? From whatever source it is derived, a sense of the intrinsic worthwhileness of individual perception and judgment is surely one of the deepest springs of intellectual vitality. The first and most essential thing that any teacher must communicate to any student is the belief that his own responses are worth making, his own thoughts worth thinking, his own judgments worth forming. The second—of equal importance—is that the world is worth exploring. Christian thought roots this double sense of worth in the conviction that it is Man's destiny to respond to God: 'the chief end of Man is to glorify God and enjoy Him for ever'. Enjoyment is the process of exploration, and if we take the enjoyment of God to include the enjoyment of His created world of nature and of man, the whole intellectual enterprise is seen as part of an expanding realm of enjoyment, since it is the nature of God to supply that which is worth responding to and the nature of Man to respond. Vitality of mind and imagination derives ultimately from belief that there is a dialogue to pursue in which both sides are real.

Of course the intellectual is only one part of the human response. This discussion has, perhaps, been slanted too exclusively on to vitality of mind, but Professor Butterfield, in passing, drops some remarks about the Fine Arts in academic communities which deserve to be pondered. The activity of enjoyment covers much more than those of analysis and criticism which are so often necessary steps towards it; it seeks an awareness in wholeness which engages the imagination and sympathy as well as the intellect. Robert Frost's words about poetry come to mind here as supplying a pattern for all intellectual and artistic activity: 'The figure a poem makes. It begins in delight and ends in wisdom.'[1] This is understood, appreciated and desired by many. What Christians can, perhaps, contribute to the academic enterprise is a conviction that this belief in the enjoyment of learning is not illusory but is built in to the very fabric of man and the universe he responds to. We are not practising a deep deception on students when we try to communicate to them the excitement of knowing. At the same time it is difficult to see how confidence in intellectual exploration can be engendered if divorced from a certain basic conviction about the meaning and worthwhileness of life as a whole.

M. R.

NOTE

[1] Robert Frost, *Complete Poems* (New York, 1949), Introduction, p. vi. I am indebted for this reference to Dr. F. Consitt.

Part Six

THE CRISIS IN ACADEMIC VOCATION

The whole of this book supposes an attitude on the part of academics which places the highest value on a combination of devotion to subject and devotion to pupils. This, of course, is not to claim that lower motives never corrupt—sins ordinary and academic have already been mentioned—but simply that the assumptions of academic life have been held to be of this high order. Ideally, it is argued, research subjects should be chosen because of a burning desire to investigate just that problem, academic appointments should go to the 'best' applicant, and, in making appointments, excellence in teaching should rank with excellence in a specialist field. Whether or no such values have ever received much more than lip-service, some would argue today that the very assumptions of academic careers are now on another level—that research is a career-jump and the choice of subject governed thereby, that getting in the right network is all-important for appointments, that time expended on any unrequired academic activities outside specialist work for publication is wasted time which earns no acknowledgment. Mrs. Floud suggests that academic teachers, coming from a background similar to their pupils', can often be 'tainted with utilitarian vocational values', playing the role of the Trojan horse within the walls. Dr. Wilson believes that the new style academic likely to be appointed in increasing numbers is a professional specialist rather than an academic teacher committed to certain fundamental values. As the pressures of an alien outside culture increase, he retreats from moral responsibility for his students into concentration upon 'his own work'. Dr. Gowenlock describes what he calls the academic rat-race and attributes mainly to this cause the departure of many prominent young post-graduates from an academic vocation:

'Academic teachers are recruited from graduate students and post-doctoral fellows. Sometimes it can be disturbing to hear the comments of these groups on the life and prospects of such teachers in Britain. These comments have relevance to our situation and also to the continuing emigration of scientists.

Occasionally some will say that they would welcome the life of an academic teacher but that the initial financial rewards make it impossible for them because they are married and are not willing to impose extra burdens on their dependants. This argument seems much less important and certainly much less revealing than another which I have heard from some obviously well-equipped to make a real contribution to academic life. This reason is the tremendous pressure of the academic 'rat-race' in Britain today. These people are not afraid of hard work, nor do I doubt their intellectual capacity; they fear that there are extra factors which will hold back their own advancement in university life. They can, of course, from their own relatively slight experience cite examples of this. One remarked to me: 'I have come to the conclusion that it is not what you know, but who you know that counts in British universities.' A man with a Ph.D. and two years' post-doctoral experience in North America could conclude that he had little chance in our system because he had done his doctoral work with a relatively unknown lecturer in a small provincial university. Had his supervisor been a professor, it might have been different, for his 'academic bank balance' would have been higher. Whenever someone is appointed to a non-advertised academic post and the 'Old Boy–Ancient University' network is held to be responsible, then the attractions of academic life are immediately devalued. Competition is not objected to; it is the element of the extra intangible (often unfair) factors that causes complaint.

'Most of the entrants will realize that there is a race to publish, since tenure has to be obtained and promotion is an attraction to normally ambitious people. Is it advisable to tackle long-term or short-term problems? Can one get the people, the facilities and the money to make a break-through in a particular field where one's ideas are good? Is it any good trying to work on a subject which is off-centre in this country and therefore too little known to be appreciated? Must one bend all one's energies towards publishing too soon and on the 'right' subject? The choice is between pursuing a genuine academic interest and joining the scramble for academic attention. Some possible future colleagues feel that they will not be able to carry out the work they want to do because of these factors, and they are not prepared to operate under such circumstances.

'Ideally a person takes up an academic pursuit because he can't do anything else. He wants to take something further and he wants to communicate it, too. The level of commitment can be very high. I knew a man between his first and second university jobs who was so much in love with his subject and with communicating it that he could not find any time to fit in girls. In time and energy the subject took up the whole of his being. But what happens to this sort of person in the rat-race? What happens, moreover, to the person who has chosen to put a great deal of himself into the work of communication rather than publication? When it comes to promotion, these imponderable qualities weigh little against an approved number of words in print.

'Those of us with years in university life may argue that this is all exaggerated, that one can overcome these factors, that we ourselves have not been prevented from exercising our own vocation as academics. That is not the point at issue. It is that these impressions are widespread and have been so for a number of years. They are derived from observation of the actual lives and attitudes of dons. Our attitudes to teaching, students, research, publication, administration, academic life, are not private but are communicated. Similarly, our attitudes to disappointment and frustration, to competition and failure, to ambition and prestige, are not confined to ourselves. They all influence our future possible colleagues.'

The warnings given to us by Mrs. Floud, Dr. Wilson and Dr. Gowenlock need to be read together. We all—some less, some more—bring into academic life the commercial and utilitarian values of our society. In the resultant clash of values it is easy to become either under-assimilated or over-assimilated to the academic tradition. The under-assimilated see no reason to concern themselves with their students' way of life and culture: as teachers they are doing a job of instruction—nothing more. The over-assimilated turn in revulsion from the attitudes and habits of students who represent a world from which they thought they had escaped. Either way—whether for utilitarian reasons or as a refined form of escape from a naughty world—the temptation is to repudiate responsibility for students and plunge into specialized scholarship. But this temptation to slip out of a situation of tension in relationships with students is frequently increased by official policies which seem to put all the weighting on the side of prestige in research. But here again the same clash of values can be discerned, for if, on the one hand, the official attitude appears to put a premium on achievements of scholarship, on the other, as Dr. Gowenlock has shown, there is a fierce jockeying for position which reveals the academic community to be permeated by the same values as the business world. The student loses out either way, and even the ideal of pure scholarship can be corroded by these influences. The enemy is within the gates and unless we do battle at all levels— in official policies, in our academic responsibilities, in our own consciences—the vocations of both scholar and teacher will succumb.

It has never been more important that we should attract into academic posts people of the right calibre and outlook, and never before have we needed so many of them. Dr. Gowenlock, therefore, raises a crucial question when he asks What image of the academic vocation are we presenting to aspirants? Even if it is conceded that the description 'rat-race for promotion' gives an over-dramatized view, there are two questions that must be put to academics. How far are we debasing the pursuit of knowledge by making it subserve career purposes? How far are we subordinating the care and teaching of students to the claims of research? The first may be left as a question put, but the second needs more discussion. It seems undoubted that ambition often drives in the direction of research rather than teaching. And for many desire does, too. Though some academics are not only 'in love with their subject', but also with communicating it, many find communication rather a bore, or only wish to carry it on at advanced levels. This can be justified, of course, on high grounds as well as low, as the following statement shows: 'We would much rather get on with our own work. "Our own work" seems immensely worth while, as a purpose calling for the devotion of a life-time, for several reasons: one is that almost any research tends to justify itself as it goes on, becoming more and more engrossing; another is that many academic teachers believe very deeply that knowledge is an absolute value, a spiritual aspiration, a non-utilitarian devotion which it is important to maintain against the materialism of the world today.' Nothing illustrates more vividly the present conflict of values in academic life than the contrast between the foregoing statement and Dr. Gowenlock's rat-race. If one is, however, committed to this in-built conviction about the worth of scholarship, then this other conflict arises, for, cutting into one's absorbtion in research, comes the working of a conscience about persons, especially students. Responsibility and concern for persons costs devastatingly in the scholar's life: it breaks and distracts thought; it necessitates crashing changes of gear; above all, it takes infinitely more in time than the outsider would suppose, since for the student with a problem time stands still and it would be hard to tell him that in fact this is not so.

It must be recognized that there is a genuine difference of focus between those academics who emphasize the excitement and importance of their subject and those who are chiefly interested in the curiosity of their pupils and the way their minds tick. This difference of outlook is not only inevitable but positively good: distinctive academic characters absorbed in their own subjects sometimes make more educational impact on students than conscientious teachers. Thus in trying to present our academic image we must allow for both types of inspiration. What is vitally important, however, is that efficient and inspired teaching should be recognized as an equally important part of the academic vocation as research. So long as we hold to our belief that teaching and research should be carried on simultaneously in the same institutions, this is the only possible position to maintain, and yet it is so seldom really believed. Time spent on undergraduates, including time spent outside formal teaching requirements, is not wasted time, yet the way promotion often goes would lead one to suppose that it was. This is not to say that, as part of their education, students should not be made to realize that their teachers have obligations to pursue research as well as to minister to their needs. But it needs to be stated emphatically that the transmission of knowledge is as important as its advancement and that it ought to be so rated in academic institutions. If promotion were more freely granted on grounds other than publication, and if recommendations for appointments stressed teaching qualifications and general services to the institution as well as research, some steps towards righting the balance would have been taken. We might also be presenting a better image of the dual academic vocation.

A teacher's vocation is, after all, a deeply human one—to help his pupils find meaning. This statement will be contested

o*   211

by many, but in varying terms it is also affirmed by many. 'Students are bewildered by the diversity of their experience, in facing such questions as, What sort of a person am I? What am I for? In the university, which is a microcosm of society, they are up against many pressures and they lack the resources and vision to cope with their freedom. Our teaching must equip people for this situation.' 'One of the things we should be trying to give students is a sense of the high privilege of being a human being. The Elizabethans understood this; hence they had lively, questioning minds. Man is unique in being a moral and rational being and something of the sense of this privilege should be got across. This should help to give a sense of whole-heartedness to what they do.' 'Students today are often like a man driving a Jaguar in third gear: we must help them to find and use more of themselves.' The 'finding of meaning' or the 'getting into top gear' can only be done by each for himself; what teachers can communicate is a sense of the worthwhileness of the search for meaning and the possibility of a satisfying answer.

M. R.

Part Seven

CONCLUSION

One of the assertions made in various ways in this book is that 'meaning' in academic studies cannot be separated from the meaning of life as a whole and that intellectual vitality stems, in part at least, from the relation of the activity of the mind to the total human experience. If the point is taken, then we must go on to ask what provision is being, or ought to be, made for this important element in higher education. The discovery of meaning involves the formation of convictions about the nature of man and the purposes of his life. It need hardly be stated that when we ask what provision is being made, we do not mean what provision for the teaching of any one orthodoxy. This would be both impossible and wrong. But is any provision being made for opportunity to discover and explore this dimension in life and for help in doing so? This question has to be asked particularly with regard to the new universities and colleges of all types now being planned and set up. A rather paradoxical situation is arising at present in that many of the older civic universities, founded in reaction against 'Theology the Queen of the Sciences', have been busy lately removing legal obstacles to the academic recognition of 'religion', while new academic institutions are being founded on the assumption that little or no such provision need be thought of, at any rate initially. Possibly, in order to avoid any taint of mere orthodoxy, institutions of higher education ought to go through a phase of leaving matters of faith on the periphery of their attention for a while, in order that they may find their own way in. But anyone who thinks deeply about the nature of the academic experience is likely to reach the conclusion that what one believes about oneself and about the world is central to one's purposes in study. 'Hollow' men or divided men cannot operate at full strength intellectually: every time one meets a student in deep difficulties this point is driven home. We simply cannot disregard this whole dimension of experience, or push it to one side as a set of questions that will somehow find answers in a haphazard fashion.

The point must be made that this question is being addressed

215

not just to Christians or religious-minded people, but to all those with responsibilities in academic institutions. It is the concern of all of us that students should not struggle along as 'hollow men' and therefore none of us can limit ourselves to a purely technical task. But what 'provision' is proper to an institution of academic learning in a heterodox society? This is the point at which we so often stick. But an inquiry into present developments, particularly in the civic universities, has revealed significant signs of a desire to make fresh provision in courses, syllabuses and teaching. These experiments can be placed in three broad categories. There are, in the first place, new courses in Christian theology and Biblical studies, often designed for the general student and to be taken in combination with other subjects. Secondly, there are indications of an increasing interest in comparative religions as a proper and important branch of academic studies. Thirdly, experiments are being made in giving fuller emphasis to the religious element in various academic fields, for example, in the study of cultures and in sociology. Beyond the undergraduate stage thought is being given to research in cross-border subjects in such fields as criminology/religion, psychology/religion, sociology/religion. These are only small signs in some places but they suggest a movement of thought towards putting more centrally in our academic attention the study of human faiths as essential to an understanding of what men do and achieve. A growing feeling on the part of teachers that we do not give a proper perspective without this is met by a growing interest among some students in the study of this aspect of civilizations.

Thus there seems a real case for a deliberate policy to put the study of religions on a new footing in higher education, that is, to make the subject no longer just the concern of a few professionally interested persons, but an element in ordinary undergraduate courses, at least on the humanities side. This might mean the extension of opportunities to take such studies as part of combined courses. It might also mean more adequate teaching of the religious elements embedded in all the humane subjects and more attention given to frontier discussions between the religious and other approaches to the study of man. To do this kind of work on a proper level of academic efficiency we need to ensure that, amid the multitude of new appointments now being made to meet expansion, some are specifically designed for these purposes. They would often need to be inter-departmental appointments. Whether such people could be recruited from among the theologians—or from the sociologists, perhaps—is a question that can only be answered by experiment. Perhaps what we want is quite a new type of theological department, a large part of whose work would be done in other departments. One of its main concerns would be to ensure that the study of what men have believed and thought about the fundamental questions of human existence throughout history should receive full and proper academic attention. There are difficulties about the use of the word theology here. We cannot make God an object of academic study nor is it appropriate for any academic institution to claim that as such it knows and can teach the truth of God. For academic institutions are bound by their techniques, which can only investigate the phenomena of nature and the activities of men, and by their proper humility which forbids them to claim to know the whole truth of anything. It seems, therefore, much more accurate to use the term Department of Religions.

So much for provision within the structure of courses and content of syllabuses. A second approach is to make provision for general and 'open' series of lectures on broad questions of human belief and conduct. This has often been done but, here again, there are some experiments going on which have a new slant. For one thing, they are sometimes organized by staff from a number of departments, including scientists and sociologists, rather than by the department of theology or philosophy alone. This is an illustration of the point we are making—that this 'search for meaning' is the serious business of many academics and not the vested interest of a few. A second significant feature is that sometimes the large-scale lecture is accompanied by a break-up into smaller discussion groups. This emphasizes the fact that no formal provision takes the place of a more intimate encounter in which questions of values and meanings can be thrashed out openly. It is, however, of real importance that formal and public provision for the treatment of such subjects should be made. The point that must be demonstrated with utmost clarity in official policies is that the institution recognizes that students study with their whole personalities and that therefore its responsibility can never be limited to intellectual processes but must always embrace concern for the whole con-

217

text of human experience in which that process takes place.

There are two other levels on which academic institutions can and perhaps ought to express their sense of the importance of ultimate questions. The first is that of individual student counselling and help. It is axiomatic in this book that academic teachers must generally be prepared to be counsellors as occasion arises, but it is also true that they are often neither adequate nor desired in this role. We have all kinds of doubts and prejudices about professional counsellors whom we suspect of creating or 'blowing up' student problems to serve their own self-importance. Yet counselling by someone is needed—of that there can be little doubt. We may continue to meet the need as casually and informally as possible, yet the facts of expansion and the problems these will create are forcing us into the position of having to make a much more conscious and organized provision for student counselling. This will have to be of various types, including psychological and religious. It is a remarkable fact that in these last years the office of a university chaplain, formerly so suspect as a relic of the ancient universities, has become a significant one in a number of civic universities. This development has only come as a response to manifest need and we must now ask urgently what kind of provision to meet this need is being made in the new universities and colleges of all types.

The other level is that of the formal provisions for religious worship and observances in academic life. Here the utmost confusion of thought and practice prevails at present. The issue meets newly founded institutions sharply, for they have to take decisions on such controversial matters as chapels, mottoes, degree ceremonies, academic sermons, and where there is no specific religious or non-religious foundation to give a directive, these things must be decided by general academic opinion. Obviously many regard any religious observances as an attempt to dress up a modern institution in the play-acting clothes of the past. It is hardly possible to expect unanimity one way or the other, and, indeed, official religious observances and gestures in academic life are so often supported for bogus reasons, that they raise many doubts. What is beginning to emerge, however, is a kind of permissive attitude which grows out of the common concerns we have been discussing in this concluding chapter. If the university or college is concerned with the whole meaning of human experience, then it must recognize that for

218

some of its members this is focused in religious worship. In that case it becomes natural and proper for an academic community to allow provision—more, to facilitate and even make provision —for the worship of its members corporately, provided always that no compulsion is exercised. It follows that the permissive right must extend to any religion. The interesting thing is that the duty of the academic institution to secure such provision of a chapel or chapels is sometimes pressed—on the kind of grounds set out above—by those who would not themselves use it. It may well be that here is the beginning of a new status of religion on the 'campus': not the old official religious observance built into the institution, nor yet the chapels and chaplaincies lining the touch-line while forbidden the actual field, but the free permissive exercise of worship as an element in the total life of the community, in a chapel which is as much part of the academic buildings as the library and laboratories but does not claim a higher place.

The last consideration brought us right up against the final question as to whether the Christian faith ought to hold a particular position in relation to higher education. The question, of course, presents itself in quite a different form to those institutions which are on a specific Christian foundation and those which are not. To the first the question is not one of right— which is clearly theirs but of how best to serve the educational objectives to which they are dedicated. It is the second form of the question which produces such bitterly opposed answers. We have tried to show that in the fundamental academic task many teachers of differing viewpoints can co-operate to see that provision is made to treat fundamental questions seriously and at a full academic level of competence. We may all agree that all the questions should be asked responsibly, but must we not also agree that all responsible answers must be allowed to stand on their own merits, with no privileged position for some? This is the old question of the academic open forum and it seems that we must reaffirm our belief that in higher education ultimate questions must be treated as open ones. But there is today a new sense of freedom to make one's contribution to the 'ultimate answers' in the fullest and most positive terms. It is as if, having pitched out privilege, Christians and others are really free to speak. We therefore feel free at this point to give three illustrations of ways in which we believe Christian thought and experience should be related to the academic enterprise and contribute towards the ultimate answers. The first point is made in a note contributed by Mr. Curling.

1. 'The perspective in which Christianity is presented to us today has a strongly existential emphasis on the theology of the person and this draws our attention away from the study of things as they are. From Kierkegaard to Buber, Brunner and Bultmann this has been strengthened until now it is suggested that "statements about God are statements about the 'ultimacy' of personal relations"[1] and even Tillich's "the ground of all being" becomes "the ground of our being". However valuable these insights may have been in the past, in an age when the claims of science are being pressed as much in the schools as in the universities, I believe we need to look again at the divine activity in creation. Cardinal Newman's defence of the university as a place of teaching universal knowledge was based on his belief that "the subject-matter of knowledge is intimately united in itself, as being the acts and the work of the Creator".[2]

'I therefore regard it as an academic and Christian responsibility to direct attention to the knowable events of common experience in all of which God is continually active. We must learn to see ourselves and others, as well as the world, as objects, as things. To know someone else as a thing may not be as bad a basis for ethics as is commonly thought. Thus the science of man should begin, not as Buber insists with the consideration of "man with man", but with man as a thing, with the examination of his flesh, of the behaviour of the molecules that constitute his living cells.

'This is a Christian responsibility because of the deep concern of Christianity with matter, to which both the manner of the Incarnation and the form of the Last Supper clearly point. The sacraments are administered in a material element not, as Aquinas suggests, because man is regrettably sensuous, but because God is gloriously sensuous. Flesh, blood, bread, wine— with these Jesus sums up the creative processes of the universe and takes to Himself the Hebrew faith that was itself grounded in matter and flesh.

'For several decades now developments in science have received little attention from theologians or philosophers. Yet even in the last few years a new image of a coinherent universe has begun to emerge in which the abundance of the elements is related to the nuclear processes in stars, and the forms of life and thought related to the information-carrying patterns of molecules. The implications of these developments are certain to be immense. Now we begin to see how passages in Colossians and Ephesians point to the coinherence and recapitulation of all things in Christ: the six-times-repeated "Ta panta" in the first chapter of Colossians is the basis of a remarkable paper by Professor Sittler calling for a Christology of nature.[3] So our task is to illumine this absorbing activity of scientific exploration by a theology of earthly reality concerned with things as they are and as they co-inhere in Christ, for all things are created and redeemed in Him.'

2. The Christian faith makes an important affirmation about the possibility of free and open inquiry. Belief in 'openness to the truth' has been a fundamental assumption of the whole academic enterprise. Unless we are convinced that preconceptions can be broken down, that minds can be receptive, that views can be changed, the ideal of the 'search for truth' is bogus. Yet the very possibility of freedom to think is under attack from various angles and students—without going deeply into the problem—often pick up enough psychological jargon to make them cynical about any claim to 'follow the truth wherever it may lead'. Doubts about the possibility of 'openness' confirm a deep desire—in the midst of so much insecurity—to remain permanently 'at home' in a comfortable, constant structure of beliefs and assumptions. We all, of course, construct such little houses for ourselves and students naturally bring theirs with them to college. They need not be shut-up little houses: new ideas may be welcomed through doors and windows, but they must accommodate themselves to the house in order to get in.

The great assumption of faith on which the academic life rests is that these houses can be modified, pulled down, rebuilt or abandoned. Its great task is to see that no student goes away with exactly the same house he brought up with him. Or perhaps, in a certain sense, it has to persuade everyone to abandon house and go on pilgrimage. This is painful, disturbing, arduous, and it is tempting to take refuge in cynicism. If we are all conditioned anyway, what is the point of trying to seek a new country in thought? We shall never really be free to go! Here Christian faith may strengthen academic faith: men can be confronted by the imperative 'Get thee up into a new country that I will show thee!' Like Abraham they may take with them a great deal of old impedimenta, but they really can get on the move when they respond in faith to the imperious confronting truth. They can commit themselves to pilgrimage and discover in the experience that openness and commitment go together. Christianity affirms, not only that God can get men out on pilgrimage, but that they can claim the courage to go on it because—whether they know it or not—they never journey beyond God. It is of burning importance today that we should affirm to students the validity of the academic call to think freely and seek to communicate to them the desire and the courage to try.

3. The place which worship occupies in the Christian life has an importance for the intellectual life. Worship—the response to infinite worth—is the very antithesis of the processes of mastery we have already discussed. It is the contemplation in wholeness of that which one is not seeking to analyse or master. It does not lead to conclusions—tidy, buttoned-up conclusions that give a feeling of security in having mastered them. Rather, worship leads to questions; it opens immense vistas where great winds may be blowing, where one is called to be exploring always but never reaching finality. It is a common fallacy to expect religion to re-create a complete pattern that ties in all the loose ends and makes sense of all. Some may even still hope that religion will supply a philosophy to reunite the academic community. Real religious thought and experience are far more likely at present to be breakers of patterns and to make nonsense. But if, intellectually, there is a painful negative work of disruption to be carried on, worship is the most positive re-creating activity that we have. It does not reshape our systems of thought but—something far more important—it kindles a common, shared imagination that can send fire racing through the mind. It is more important to share this sense of the glory of God and the worth it imparts to all things than to lay out tidy systems of belief and try to contain our minds within them.

M. R.

NOTES

1. J. A. T. Robinson, *Honest to God* (London, 1963), p. 50.
2. J. H. Newman, *The Idea of a University* (London, 1873), p. 99.
3. Given at the 1961 Assembly of the World Council of Churches, printed in the *Ecumenical Review*, vol. 14, pp. 177–87.

Is a Christian Appraisal of Higher Education Possible?

JAMES BLACKIE

Is there a Christian appraisal of higher education which is distinctive from the humanist or the political? The essays in this book show that both the Christian and the non-Christian involved in the university world share to a considerable extent fundamental views about the aims of higher education and the weaknesses in the present system. This may seem surprising to some people who imagine that the nineteenth-century controversies between science, philosophy and religion have left an unbridgeable gap in terms of ends as well as method. Questions about the nature of acceptable evidence and the analysis of language still occasion discussion in senior common-rooms; occasional discussion of them, in fact, provides a good illustration of the academic community at its work, but I doubt if any but the more dogmatic and possibly older amongst Christians and Humanists sees his first task as the attack of the other's point of view. In my experience, the paths of Christian and Humanist in the academic life of the 50's and 60's lead not to head-on collision but to a parallel concern.

It is perhaps only those outside this community who desire to hear a clear Christian voice saying different things from the Humanist or the politican. But what would they like to hear? In terms of so-called 'lower' education the churches seem to have said little that was original about education since the passing of the Education Act in 1944, except perhaps to insist that religious instruction should remain in the school syllabus, or that the daily assembly must include prayers. This demand could never be made of universities. Indeed, with the possible exception of the occasional request for more Departments of

Theology or permission asked of university authorities for chaplains to work amongst students, the Churches have not involved themselves in the discussion about the aims and methods of higher education.

The kind of discussion which has been exciting universities in the past five years has been mainly confined to consideration of practical issues, e.g. the desirability of a purely residential academic community or the kind of provision for welfare agencies to cope with students' problems. But now suddenly it seems that, confronted with a new situation of rapid expansion and great opportunity, some basic thoughts on the aims of education are being voiced publicly, even if in a tentative manner.

What are the essential aims which are emerging from the discussion? There is agreement on the need to educate the so-called 'whole' man, however this may be interpreted in practical terms; there is agreement on the need to encourage a proper motivation for learning, to communicate the values of the past, to discriminate the essential from the peripheral in the present and to advance the boundaries of knowledge for the future, and, over all, to relate the fruits of knowledge to the community in terms of service and insight.

If these then are agreed, what is the specific Christian contribution that can add to them or put them in a different context?

Many would want to argue that these educational values have sprung directly from the Western cultural tradition, still impregnated by Christian presuppositions although rejecting much of the framework. These aims and thoughts *are* Christian and any appraisal can be made only from within the academic community, where labels or allegiances are irrelevant.

Yet perhaps this is too simple a view of the effect of one's presuppositions on practical issues. These issues will arise again and again in urgent terms concerning the kind of universities which will be created in the next twenty or so years, and the way in which we operate the process of learning and acquiring technological skills. It may be that the same answer from Christians and the rest will usually be given to these problems. The importance of the personal in the learning process, and the necessity of inquiry which is free and unfettered are only two examples of this agreement in the present situation. But this is not to release the Christian from the obligation to examine carefully and reflect continually on the basis of his judgments and attitudes, and its relation to the faith which he professes. This is saying no more than is demanded of all those engaged in higher education. The examination of hidden presuppositions, bias and the springs of prejudice is an academic necessity, and for the Christian, it is, in fact, 'built-in' to the gospel.

Perhaps a start can be made with the witness to that aspect of reality which is described in various ways in various contexts and is in theological terms denoted by the word 'spiritual'. Christianity has always proclaimed this aspect, not in impersonal terms, but in relation to a Person, who has been described in theological terms, as having 'two natures in one person'. Within the strictly limited theological framework in which it is stated, it is sometimes asked how this assertion can have anything to do with the form and curriculum of a modern university, except in terms of its influence on history. This is an important question, admitting of no easy and direct answer. Yet this theological witness has provided the spring of inspiration and insight when understood as describing a particular aspect of the situations in which men must live and work. Historically, art, music, literature and science have all received dynamic inspiration from the way in which this witness or description has been seen to be relevant and urgent in particular situations.

It is the theological description of the relation between the unseen and the seen, when used as a tool, that can often illuminate contemporary problems. Some of these relate to the nature of man and his potentiality in educational terms. What are we seeking for him and from him in our universities? Is the controversy about the 'two cultures' not another way of describing the situation that was once spoken of in the theological terms of 'spirit' and 'flesh'?

And what about the concept of commitment? Probably this is the one aspect of higher education that has been explored in the most thorough manner in recent years, beginning from Sir Walter Moberley's book, *The Crisis in the University* (1949). It could be argued again that the theological method, with its demand for engagement with the Object of study before true learning begins, provided an illuminating model for other academic disciplines which were suffering from a mystique of liberal open-mindedness and which had run-down to a kind of non-committed 'dilettantism'. What Moberley did, was not to demand a new approach, but rather, to draw out in articulation what, in fact, was happening already. By using his theological model in this way he was able to delineate the actual situation and methods employed by the dedicated scientist or to suggest the approach to his subject to be taken by a first-year historian.

As has been said already, this may mean that the insights gained by this method are the same as those arrived at by others of different persuasions. This is to be welcomed. But it does not mean that this will always be so. Indeed there is a clear strand in the gospel which indicates that it ought not to be so. Crucifixion is at the heart of all things and can be expected, though not sought for its own sake.

For the Christian, the demand is continually laid upon him, to reflect on this gospel, even though no easy connection can be made in terms of immediate action. This is perhaps the meaning of faith in the academic community. By waiting upon the Word we are in a position of expectancy and hope. In this revolutionary expanding situation, it is perhaps easier for Christians to accept the death of the old and traditional idea of the university and look for the rebirth of institutions of learning open to all who have ability. They should also be waiting for the sound of new explosions of knowledge and amongst all the demolition work discern something of the form of the Christ in whom, as the letter to the Colossians states, 'lie hidden all God's treasures of wisdom and knowledge'.